ROCK
Making Musical Choices

Richard Peck

BOB JONES UNIVERSITY PRESS
GREENVILLE, SOUTH CAROLINA 29614

Rock: Making Musical Choices
by Richard Peck
© 1985 Bob Jones University Press
Greenville, SC 29614
ISBN: 0-89084-297-3

Printed in the United States of America

To Susie, Kris, and Bob
Romans 12:2

Contents

Acknowledgments

In a sense, this book was begun almost ten years ago. A concerned pastor encouraged me to think about my music and to examine it based upon the Bible's standards. Since that time, God has used many other godly Christians to shape the content of this project.

To thank all of them would be impossible. However, I owe a special debt to the members of the administration, faculty, staff, and student body of Bob Jones University. I am especially grateful to Dr. Bob Jones III for his encouragement and helpful suggestions. Similarly, I am indebted to Dr. Dwight Gustafson, dean of the School of Fine Arts, for his support and his very perceptive review of the manuscript.

I am also grateful to Mr. Robert Franklin, managing editor of *FAITH for the Family*, and to his staff. In addition to handling the publication of this book, they provided encouragement, forwarded clippings, and located sources of information that contributed to the completeness and accuracy of the manuscript.

Numerous other Christian colleagues were kind enough to take time to help. I especially appreciated the work of Doug Manor, David Warren, and Bruce Cox of the Fine Arts faculty, who read the manuscript and suggested ways to strengthen it. I also received valuable assistance from Ross Penix and Craig Olsen of Bob Jones Academy. Several co-laborers at Bob Jones University Press dedicated personal time to the project, including Susan Bunker, George Collins, Freddie Creason, Donna Hess, Brian Johnson, and Sandy Stock. Their help and encouragement were invaluable, and I owe them many thanks. The opportunity to talk with several groups of students also sharpened the book's focus, and the willingness of these students to ask questions and share their experiences with me was very helpful.

Finally, the book could not have been completed without the help of Bill and Joan Pinkston and my family. The Pinkstons reviewed several drafts of almost every chapter. They contributed so much to the concept and structure of the book, that it would be nearly impossible to separate their work from my own. My wife and children cheerfully transcribed reviewers' comments, helped with typing, and gave up the family time necessary for me to complete this project. Without their patience, prayer, and support, the work would not have been possible.

Introduction

. . . was blind, but now I see.
—from *Amazing Grace* by John Newton

Why publish another book about rock? Hasn't it all been said, both for and against rock, by its admirers and critics?

The answer is no. The music has changed, of course. The songs of the fifties are just a historical footnote to today's videos. But the rock movement that began three decades ago is still one of the most powerful cultural forces in the world. Unfortunately, much of that power is being used to challenge biblical standards. Rock has become a Goliath-sized industry capable of setting musical—and even visual—trends for the entire world.

However, while rock has gotten worse, its critics have grown silent. Some secular organizations, such as the National Coalition on Television Violence, *are* worried about the sadistic, evil themes that are typical of many new rock videos. But the NCTV is largely concerned about rock that is anti-social, not anti-God.

Christians who speak out against rock find themselves condemned by the world and by other Christians. Even those who do see the problems with rock often have trouble with the "gray" areas—music that falls somewhere between the extremes. What about rock with no words? And what about Christian rock or "CCM" (contemporary Christian music)?

The purpose of this book is to help the Christian establish a proper perspective on contemporary music. Much of the information in the book is confirmed by first-hand experience. Like many young people, I loved rock. I listened to rock, owned hundreds of albums, and attended rock concerts. Like some, I was also a rock performer. As a member of six groups over twelve years, I sang, played, and recorded rock music.

Performance was followed by publishing. The company I was with is now one of the top pop copyright publishers in America. Not long ago, twenty of *Billboard's* Hot 100 were controlled by this firm—with three in the top ten! I was also a member of NARAS (the National Academy of Recording Arts and Sciences) and participated in the voting for the Grammy Awards each year. That same company was active in CCM. During the last two years I was with the company, I worked with a number of commercially successful CCM executives and performers.

This experience with contemporary music is not desirable. If those years could be repeated, I would not live them in the same way. Paul seems to have had this feeling about his years as a Pharisee. Nevertheless, in Philippians, he reviews his credentials just to make the point with his readers that he had *seen* the best that Judaism had to offer but found no satisfaction. [1] I hope that, through this book, you will see that the same can be said for contemporary music.

Finally, keep in mind that this book is written from the perspective of a Bible-believing Christian. If you are not saved, if you do not believe the Bible, you will find some points in this book puzzling. To have a proper perspective on rock, you must have a proper view of Christ.

As you read, ask yourself, "Am I open to God's direction about rock?" When Christ restored the sight of the blind man, the Pharisees chose to remain "blind"—refusing to believe the personal testimony of the man who had been healed. [2]

Like the Pharisees, all of us are spiritually blind from birth. If your attitude resembles theirs, ask God to open your spiritual eyes. He has promised to instruct you, to teach you, and to guide you. [3] Prove Him faithful to that promise.

Endnotes

1. Philippians 3:4-7.

2. John 9.

3. Psalm 32:8.

Section One:
Goliath's Challenge

Everybody hates a bully. The boy who says his dad can lick your dad, the muscle-bound hunk who kicks sand in the little guy's face at the beach, the wolf at the door of the three little pigs—these are legendary bullies.

But not all bullies exist only in legend. When Goliath strode into the valley of Elah, the armies of Israel trembled. "Choose you a man ...," he shouted, "and let him come down to me" (I Samuel 17:8). And the men of Israel fled from him. Only David stood, saying, "Is there not a cause?" David realized that Goliath was not simply mocking the men of Israel: he was mocking the God of Israel as well.

Is there not a cause *today,* as a Goliath-sized industry pours out record after record praising sin and Satan? Is there not a cause, as MTV (Music Television) rocks sets across America with twenty-four-hour violence and perversion? Have we as Christians forgotten that we are to "war a good warfare" against sin (I Timothy 1:18)? Or is rock only the jolly green giant, as some would have us believe?

Rock: Making Musical Choices looks at contemporary music and seeks honest answers for the Christian.

We've Heard It All Before

1

We have heard this over and over until I am sick. I know rock and roll is wrong. [But] what about artists whose words don't say anything wrong? This is the hard issue today, or what about music . . . with no words?
—A Christian college student

Drugs, immorality, satanic lyrics, backward masking—you've heard it all before. Meanwhile, books and lectures about rock continue to warn that rock kills plants; rock will damage your hearing; rock's low frequencies affect your heart rate and body metabolism; the music bypasses your brain's conscious control centers, and the rhythm stimulates immoral desires. You've heard all of this, too.

What you may *not* have heard is that the real issue is holiness. The word is seldom used today, but the Bible makes it clear that Christians are to be a holy people. They are to be separated from the world unto God. [1]

By talking about houseplants, hearing, and heart rates—instead of holiness—far too much discussion of rock has focused on rock's effects upon man rather than its offensiveness to God. The result is that many are more interested in what God might *permit* than in how He might be *pleased.*

The questions young people ask about rock often demonstrate this. "Do you think it would be all right if ... ?" Or, "Do you see anything wrong with ... ?"

Asking for advice is fine. But these questions, like many of the usual arguments against rock, miss the point. The key is not what I think about rock or what you think about rock. The question is "What does God think about rock?" That is the issue. That is the question this book seeks to answer.

What Does God Expect?

If you are a Christian, you've asked God to accept you into a relationship that will last forever. There was a time in your life when you realized that your sin had offended Him. You also realized that the penalty for sin is death. [2] But Christ died to pay that penalty, and by expressing sorrow for your sin and asking God to accept you on the basis of Christ's shed blood, you entered into an eternal relationship. [3]

How do we know these things are true? Because the Bible says so. And the Bible says your life is to be changed after you have entered into that relationship. The apostle Paul explained this to the early Christians at Ephesus and Rome:

> In time past ye walked according to the course of this world ... fulfilling the desires of the flesh and of the mind; ... But God, who is rich in mercy ... hath quickened us [made us alive] together with Christ. [4] ... so we also should walk in newness of life. [5]

To walk in newness of life affects *everything* you do. It should affect your clothing, your conduct when you are with friends and when you are alone, your conversations and your thoughts—and even your music!

Three Types of Readers

What's your opinion of contemporary music? How

much do you know about it? What position, if any, do your friends encourage you to take toward this music? What do your parents think about rock? Probably most people reading this book fit into one of the three following categories:

Group 1	Group 2	Group 3
You listen to rock regularly and see nothing wrong with it.	You are aware of the problems with rock, but seriously question the validity of some criticisms of rock.	You've had almost no exposure to rock and would have difficulty discussing it intelligently.

A Word to the First Group. Quite often, those who *really* see nothing wrong with rock have not truly accepted Christ as their Saviour. If you feel no uneasiness in seeing Christ mocked, hearing God's name used in a blasphemous way, and watching popular groups exalt Satan, you should be concerned for your soul.

On the other hand, if you have accepted Christ, there are several possible reasons why you see nothing wrong with rock music. The first is that the old arguments against rock have not been convincing. Your plants are alive and well, you haven't lost your hearing, and your heart rate seems to be fine. However, please realize that you still have a responsibility to find out the truth about contemporary music—and not simply to react to its critics.

Or possibly you think (perhaps even unconsciously) that dabbling with rock is a way to express your maturity. "I'm old enough to investigate and make choices for myself." The information in this book will help you make an intelligent decision about music. However, as you learn more about contemporary music, you may find that in some cases, you haven't been making your own choices at all!

Finally, some listen to rock as a deliberate act of rebellion. Remember David's prayer, "Against thee, thee only, have I sinned, and done this evil in thy sight." [6] David was guilty of adultery and murder, sins against mankind, yet he realized his greatest sin was against God. You may think your rebellion is directed toward your parents or your school, but, like David, your most serious sin is against God.

To the Second Group. You're selective about contemporary music. You know the difference between serious musical efforts and musical junk. Probably you feel that, with care, you can enjoy the good and avoid any negative effects of the bad.

Don't just scan this book. Pay particularly close attention to the Bible's teaching about separation and association. The Christian is to avoid even the appearance of evil [7] and must sometimes be willing to sacrifice his own interests for the sake of others. "We then that are strong ought to bear the infirmities of the weak, and not to please ourselves." [8]

To the Third Group. You are in a minority. In fact, you are probably reading this book in hopes of helping someone else. If so, be aware that neither this book nor any other will make you an expert on contemporary music.

In talking about rock, be quick to admit you have little firsthand experience with rock. A reasonable person will understand it is not necessary for you to have burned your hand to find out that the stove is hot.

God changes lives; we don't. Something you say to a friend who is involved with rock may have an effect months or even years later. Meanwhile, pray that God will work on behalf of that person for whom you are concerned.

A Word to All

Most of us, at one time or another, find someone else trying to influence us about music. For instance, I am trying to influence you through this book. The great difference is, however, that I would rather have you seeking the *Lord's* direction than mindlessly adopting my position.

Remember that at the beginning of this section I asked, "What's *your* opinion of contemporary music?" You need to be aware of the forces that are seeking to shape your thinking.

Friends influence us, whether intentionally or not. Many young people listen to rock because it seems that all of their friends do. The record industry would also like to influence you: it spends millions of dollars each year to affect your choices. Finally, the society around you can have an influence—through newspapers and magazines, through television, through advertising, and more—and that society is being strongly influenced by the rock subculture.

When all is said and done, the choice is yours; the Lord will hold *you* responsible for what music you choose. However, unless you are careful, this choice will not even be your own, much less be consistent with God's will for your life. If you haven't weighed the issues carefully, you need to do so.

Endnotes

1. Psalm 1:1; I John 2:3-6.

2. Romans 3:23; Romans 6:23.

3. Titus 3:3-7.

4. Ephesians 2:2-5.

5. Romans 6:4.

6. Psalm 51:4a.

7. I Thessalonians 5:22.

8. Romans 15:1.

What Is Rock?
2

Rock and Roll: The term is a blues euphemism for sexual intercourse.
—The Rolling Stone Encyclopedia of Rock and Roll

Rock cannot be described with a simple musical definition. For example, *Billboard* magazine[1] publishes at least nine different charts, including:

—The Hot 100	—Hot Latin LP's
—Adult Contemporary	—Hot Country
—Black Singles	—Inspirational LP's
—Rock Albums	—Videocassettes
—Dance/Disco	

Other charts are sometimes added to this list. And while these charts make some useful commercial distinctions, they don't do much to help us define rock. For example, some country music sounds like rock; some rock sounds like country. The same can often be said of black music and rock, latin music and rock, adult contemporary and rock, and most other categories. To make matters worse, popular songs frequently appear on more than one chart (the record industry calls this "crossover").

The point is this: as we begin this chapter, you

need to understand that there is no single, universally accepted, musical definition of rock. Certain writers, particularly critics of rock, have tried to suggest definitions. "It always has a strong beat," some say. Others add, "Rock is characterized by repetition." Still others may stress specific patterns of meter, certain chord progressions, and more.

"After all," some might think, "it hasn't been effective just to tell young people that rock is wrong. But if we could just convince the kids that rock will kill their plants, or that they'll lose their hearing . . . or that the subsonic frequencies will affect their heart rates— *everybody* is interested in fitness!"

The result of this process is that those of us who are concerned about rock have spent far too much time focusing on arguments that appeal solely to the listeners' own selfish interests. Ought not our primary desire be Christlikeness? If so, our most compelling argument against rock is that the Bible teaches us to be separated from sin unto God.

Even this argument could be abused by waving it like a flag to conceal a poorly constructed case against rock. But the next three chapters will show that contemporary music has built a convincing case against itself. Christians don't need to rely on flag-waving or foggy definitions.

The Lumpers and the Dividers

However, despite the difficulty that exists in defining rock, we need ground rules for the use of the word in this book so that you will know what I'm talking about. Not surprisingly, one of the biggest obstacles in discussing rock is vocabulary. For some, *rock* has a very specific meaning. For others, usually those who did not grow up listening to rock, the term means almost anything recorded since 1950. Probably *no* one intends to convey (or even remembers) the original definition of rock cited at the beginning of this chapter.

Instead, when we talk about rock today, two groups of people seem to emerge—the *lumpers* and the *dividers.* The lumpers are usually critical of rock. You will hear them make statements like, "All rock is noise," or "I don't know how you listen to that junk." While the lumpers are really trying to help, labeling all rock as musical garbage only makes matters worse. Most young people know that there are some very talented songwriters and musicians performing contemporary music. A case can be made against rock, but it won't be on the grounds that everything recorded since Brahms's century is noise.

On the other hand, many defenders of rock tend to be dividers. A divider will usually try to carve contemporary music into a number of slices—each one thinner than the last. This technique is sometimes heard when a divider is answering someone who has attacked rock. "I don't really like rock," the divider will say. "I listen to _____" (fill in the blank).

One person fills the blank with "soft rock," while another says "new wave," and yet another "contemporary Christian music." Maybe Mom *doesn't* know the difference between Van Halen and Amy Grant. However, to hide rock's problems behind a set of exotic labels is no more honest or useful than some critics' eagerness to lump all rock together into one big category called noise.

How Will the Term "Rock" Be Used in This Book?

Despite the differences, unless only *one* type of music is being discussed, it is usually easier just to say rock. In this book, that is how the word *rock* will be used. To discuss a particular style, of course, the proper label for that style will be used.

For variety, I'll also use the terms *contemporary music* and *popular music.* All that really matters is that *you* know how I am using these terms. As you'll soon see, past attempts to pin rock to a precise musical formula have sometimes done more harm than good. For the purposes of this book, the simple, conversational sense of the word will serve well.

Popular Misconceptions

Before finishing this chapter, let's be sure we agree on what rock is *not.* This quick survey of common misconceptions about rock may prove useful. Be sure to pay particularly close attention to these if you are among that third group of readers, the ones with little or no first-hand exposure to contemporary music.

Misconception 1: All rock is three-chord musical rubbish. We touched on this earlier in discussing the lumpers and the dividers. The assertion that all rock musicians are untrained and untalented cannot be supported. Beginning as early as the seventies, there were several groups who established reputations for top quality musicianship. Emerson, Lake, and Palmer's *Works* album even features an original piano concerto and the London Philharmonic Orchestra, along with contemporary settings of Copland's *Fanfare for the Common Man* and a Bach two-part invention. An earlier Emerson, Lake, and Palmer album was based on Mussorgsky's *Pictures at an Exhibition.* Other examples of such professionalism include Yes, Chicago, Steely Dan, and Blood, Sweat, and Tears.

Vocal harmonies of groups like Crosby, Stills, and Nash developed at the same time other groups were demonstrating quality musicianship. Studio techniques progressed with the performers. Electronic music synthesizers appeared. Complex twenty-four, thirty-two, and even sixty-four track recorders began to produce elaborate "layered" recordings. The technical quality of most contemporary recordings is outstanding.

Yes, some rock is noise. Some performers boast of never having played an instrument until they joined a band. For example, poor musicianship is almost a basic requirement of punk rock. But punk is a reaction against order and society, so it's natural that little emphasis would be placed on technique. The generalization that *all* rock is noise simply isn't true and has probably done more to discredit well-meaning critics of rock than any of the other misconceptions that follow.

Misconception 2: Rock lyrics always focus on sex, drugs, and violence. The key word is "always." It's true that the words to the popular songs are often offensive or obscene. However, the songwriting abilities of performers such as Barry Manilow, Paul McCartney, Carole King, Stevie Wonder, and others established that contemporary composers could blend music and text to create melodic, memorable songs. The problem, as discussed in the next chapter, is that the Christian has no way to find the few memorable songs that may be written without exposing himself or herself to the bad ones as well. Even if there were a sanitized Hot 100 for Christians, the problems of association (discussed in chapters four, five, and six) would remain.

Misconception 3: The kids will grow out of rock. They won't! Without God's help, those of us who grew up with contemporary music only "grow" in the sense of developing more sophisticated tastes for the same type of music.

To expect a totally unprompted reversal of the musical tastes held by an entire generation is simply not realistic. There is no more cause to expect rock fans to "grow out of it" than there is to expect a child raised on meat-and-potatoes suddenly to give it up for a diet of raw fish. Whether fish is better or worse is not the issue; it's different, and long-established preferences usually change slowly.

Misconception 4: Rock is dying. Rock is healthier than ever before. The future of popular music has been cloudy at times, but only because a superstar or some major trend was fading without a clear successor. Still, Elvis was replaced. So were the Beatles. AM radio gave way to FM and album-oriented rock (AOR) stations. It now appears that it may be FM's turn to make way for TV. Musicvideos offer the brightest hope the record industry has had in years. In fact, the video phenomenon is so important that all of chapter four is devoted to MTV and its look-alikes.

* * * * *

Before closing chapter two, let's preview where we are headed. In chapter three, we'll look at some of the trends in contemporary music. Who are the important figures in the world of rock? How do they live? What do they believe? What message, if any, does their music present? Then, in chapter four, we'll focus on one fact that should be particularly disturbing to the Christian: the open promotion of satanism by a number of groups. Regardless of whether these groups are sincere in exalting Satan or are doing so simply for its shock value, there is no place for such performers in the Christian's life.

Chapter five discusses the video revolution. For the first time since rock was born we can now *see* through these musicvideos what occupies the thoughts and the minds of rock composers and performers. Since visual communication is so much more powerful than simple recordings, the Christian needs to know what these performers are thinking. The Bible says that "out of the abundance of the heart the mouth speaketh." [2] That which is in the hearts of many contemporary performers is now being broadcast into our homes on the television screen.

Chapter six closes the first section of the book. In that chapter, we will sum up our discussion of rock before turning to contemporary Christian music. Our objective in chapter six will be to look at God's message concerning rock with the aim of finding a clear, scriptural basis for making sound decisions about contemporary music. That foundation will also help us as we turn to CCM in section two.

Endnotes

1. *Billboard* is the most important trade magazine of the record industry.

2. Matthew 12:34.

Pizza or Poison?
3

[Rock] is the total celebration of the physical. [1]
—**Ted Nugent**

How accurate is that image? Critics are quick to call rock physical, but Ted Nugent is a rock performer, a person who ought to know. Are the critics on target when they claim that rock promotes immoral physical desires and that the lifestyle of many groups should cause the Christian concern?

"No!" many respond. "It isn't fair! *I* don't live like that, and I don't even listen to the lyrics. I just like the music. Besides, what's wrong with the good groups? Can't I listen to the good groups and ignore the bad ones?"

This question raises the issue of "discernment" or "selectivity." By the power of the Holy Spirit, Christians have the ability to discern between good and evil. [2] Christians also have a unique source of strength in Christ. [3] As a result, some rock fans have suggested that Christian young people should reevaluate their approach to contemporary music. "Instead of tossing out all the music we hear on radio and MTV," the argument goes, "we show greater spiritual maturity by enjoying the good and rejecting the bad."

To help explain what's wrong with this thinking, let's set up an analogy. An analogy is a comparison, pointing out some likeness in two things that are being compared.

Pizza or Food Poisoning?

Close your eyes and imagine yourself at home. Gradually you realize you're getting hungry. What do you do? Head to the kitchen for a snack? Or, better yet, make a quick trip down the street to your favorite hamburger place? Probably so.

But imagine yourself arriving at that hamburger place and heading for the dumpster instead of the cash registers! Rooting around through all the trash, you find a pretty good bun and an almost complete hamburger patty. "Ah," you exclaim, "I've discerned the good from the bad, and now I will enjoy my meal!"

Or picture yourself and a group of friends who are hungry for pizza. Where are you going to get it—in your favorite pizza restaurant or out behind the place by going through their dumpster? It depends on whether you want pizza or food poisoning.

Ridiculous analogies, yes, but they are not far from the approach some rock fans take to justify contemporary music. What is the comparison these analogies make? Christians who want to listen to the "good" music that is mixed in with the bad are like hungry people trying to find good food mixed in with the trash. There is nourishment in leftovers, just as there is some good-sounding contemporary music. But do we go to the garbage to be fed? No. Even the "good" food that we might find has been contaminated by the garbage that surrounds it. As a result, we run the risk of food poisoning, even though we shun the bad and look for the good.

The apostle Paul, writing under the inspiration of the Holy Spirit, pointed out that Christians cannot walk in the midst of sinful pleasures—no matter how much discernment and strength we may have in Christ.

> What shall we say then? Shall we continue in sin, that grace may abound? God forbid. How shall we that are dead to sin, live any longer therein? [4]

In Psalm 40, verse two, David tells us the same thing: "[God] brought me up . . . out of an horrible pit, out of the miry clay." When a Christian tries to be "selective" about rock, he or she leaps into the pit.

Maybe you still don't see the connection. Or perhaps you think that the analogy is unfair. Don't decide just yet. As you read, I think you'll see that the Christian involved with rock has chosen an alternative worse than pizza or food poisoning.

Violence

Black and Blue, the title of a 1976 album by The Rolling Stones, was one of the first warnings of the direction many groups would take for the 1980s. By the mid-1970s, brutality and violence had become a full-fledged part of the Stones' act. Although *Black and Blue* received public criticism for its battered-woman advertising campaign, few people saw how prophetic the theme would prove to be.

Today, one of the primary concerns of the National Coalition on Television Violence is the sexual and sadistic violence of rock musicvideos. In fact, many performers appear to attract violence—and, some say, invite it. The Rolling Stones Altamont concert at which a listener was stabbed to death by the Hell's Angels is well known. Other performers' casual attitudes toward violence are less well known.

"My philosophy is two eyes for an eye," Ted Nugent said in the same interview quoted at the beginning of this chapter. "There was this kid in England who kept reaching over the stage and knocking my microphone into my mouth while I was singing. I forgave him maybe ten times. Then I slammed the mike stand into his face and smashed his nose. The blood was streaming down, and he sort of disappeared into the crowd." [5]

This violence is not always outwardly directed. Terry Kath of the popular rock group Chicago died from a self-inflicted gunshot wound. John Lennon was shot outside his apartment building in New York. Peter Ham of Badfinger hanged himself. Graham Bond was found dead under the wheels of a train. Yet death, knives, and firearms are frequent musicvideo themes.

We'll look at violence again in chapter four. The important point here, as we survey the current trends in rock, is to see that violence in rock is neither new nor limited to one or two well-known groups.

False Religion

More than one observer of the rock scene has suggested that the rock concerts are closer to religious events than to entertainment. "That's the real reason for either rock or country concerts," suggested one writer. "They're the religious ceremonies of a nonreligious age." [6]

What do the musicians and singers themselves say? What's their view? Early performers, like Elvis Presley and Jerry Lee Lewis, professed to be Christian, although their lives seldom showed any evidence of their faith. However, more recent performers take a different view of spiritual things. "Religion makes me want to [*obscenity*] . I'm bowing to me. There's nothing spiritual about it." [7] Others agree. "I don't care about souls . . . . See, I take a real cold view about that stuff." [8]

If rock's view of religion consisted of only a cold stare, it would be sad but far less dangerous. Many performers, however, are religious *and* are eager to share their beliefs. The problem is that virtually all of these performers hold the wrong beliefs. Cults and false religions of every type abound.

One such religion that has received publicity for its connection with certain rock performers is Transcendental Meditation, often referred to by the initials TM. Although thinly disguised as a nonreligious "technique" for removing stress, it is a cult headed by the Maharishi Mahesh Yogi. Although he avoids calling it a religion, it has its origins in Hinduism. In addition, the Maharishi (Sanskrit for "great sage") has said that his idea is "the regeneration of the whole world through meditation." His followers speak of him in terms that would be more appropriate for Christ. One TM disciple said that the Maharishi's "coming to us must be considered an act of self-sacrifice." [9]

Early TM enthusiasts included groups as popular as Fleetwood Mac, the Beach Boys, and the Beatles. The Beatles began dabbling with TM a year or so following John Lennon's now famous remark, "Christianity will go . . . We're more popular than Jesus Christ right now." A decade later popular performers were still disciples of TM. "We believe in it," said Brian Wilson of the Beach Boys. "We feel it's our responsibility, partially, to carry the Maharishi message into the world." [10]

Other eastern religions have always had a following among rock performers. Buddhism, Hinduism, Krishna, and Bahaism have been particularly popular. Performers who have been involved with these and other Eastern religions include Yes, Police, Todd Rundgren, David Bowie, Neil Diamond, George Harrison, the Moody Blues, Seals and Croft, Gary Wright, The Who, and many others.

This would be reason enough for concern. However, the strongest "religious" trend is actually toward glorification of Satan and open blasphemy of God. Because this satanic emphasis is so widespread, chapter four examines this trend in more detail.

Materialism and Self-Indulgence

Rock superstars live like kings. So extravagant is their lifestyle that one European record industry executive dubbed them "the last royalty." In a century when queens, presidents, and heads-of-state have curbed spending habits to avoid criticism, popular music idols satisfy their smallest whims—spending more on one concert tour than whole families will earn in a lifetime.

Certainly, this extravagance is not limited to rock stars. Country singers, TV performers, and even popular athletes are often guilty of the same sin. But we are concerned here with rock and with whether the Christian should support the self-indulgent lifestyle of today's performers. When we buy record albums and attend concerts by contemporary performers, we use the Lord's money to do that very thing.

Diana Ross's two "free" concerts in Manhattan's Central Park (for the purpose of raising money to help build a children's playground) cost $2.5 million to stage—an amount that shocked New Yorkers and even led non-Christians to question the "imperial style and spending habits" of contemporary music's superstars. [11] Limousines, catered food, and air travel exceeded $100,000 for the two-night event. More money was spent to erect the stage and scaffolding than the purchase price of an above-average American home. Ross's costume alone cost over $11,000.

Even so, some associated with the concerts said

Ross's tastes were simple compared with other super-stars. Led Zeppelin's tours often shunned commercial airlines in favor of their own jet aircraft chartered at fees of $2,500 per hour.[12] Before his death in 1977, however, Elvis Presley was one up on most other performers. His four-engine Convair 880 jet was a ninety-six passenger plane purchased from Delta and converted into a near-replica of *Air Force One* (the plane flown by the President of the United States).[13]

What permits—even encourages—these expenditures? As *New York* magazine said of Ross, "As a star, she has acquired certain prerogatives." This notion is not Ross's only. Groups seem to compete to see whose attorney can write the most outlandish contract riders (conditions other than monetary payment necessary to secure the services of a group). Private dressing rooms with well-stocked refrigerators and bars are standard. Some go further. Van Halen reportedly likes M & M's but demands that the brown ones be removed from the bags![14]

Newer groups may not have the cash flow required to support such extravagance, but almost all of them hope to reach a level of popularity that will make it possible. Meanwhile, they leave a trail of littered or smashed hotel rooms, defiled groupies,[15] and empty liquor bottles and drug syringes.

Drugs

Given the number of deaths among rock performers, it is amazing that drug use continues. This is a partial list of only the better-known rock figures who have died as a result of drug- or alcohol-related incidents:

Janis Joplin	Sid Vicious (The Sex Pistols)
Tim Hardin	John Bonham (Led Zeppelin)

Tim Buckley	John Belushi ("Saturday Night
Elvis Presley	Live" and The Blues Brothers)
Jimi Hendrix	Tommy Bolin (Deep Purple)
Gram Parsons	Brian Jones (The Rolling Stones)
Keith Moon (The Who)	Robbie McIntosh
Bon Scott (AC/DC)	(Average White Band)
Jim Morrison	Brian Cole (The Association)
(The Doors)	Alan Wilson (Canned Heat)

By some reports, more than eighty performers in top groups over the past twenty years have died in drug-related incidents. Despite this, others continue to use and recommend drugs.

The list of arrests and those who admit drug use would run several more pages. Snorting cocaine is routine, even fashionable. Marijuana is hardly viewed as a "drug." Uppers and downers for every occasion are almost a required item. Even heroin is no longer regarded as the addictive narcotic that it is; it is enjoying increased popularity.

In some ways, the attitude of today's performers toward drugs is more dangerous than it was during the late 1960s and the 1970s. Although there was more open discussion and obvious rebellion in using drugs during the era of the San Francisco "flower child," LSD, and *Sergeant Pepper's Lonely Hearts Club Band*, the matter-of-factness associated with drug use in the 1980s is frightening. The Christian's mind and life are to be under the control of the Holy Spirit. Paul told the Ephesians, "Be not drunk with wine . . . but be filled with the Spirit." [16] The Christian cannot become casual or indifferent to this increasing acceptance of drug use.

Sex

Name the punk band that features an ex-topless dancer as lead singer and is managed by a promoter who reportedly produced porn shows in New York (after earning a master's degree in fine arts from a major Ivy League university).

If you answered The Plasmatics, you follow rock closely or you were in Milwaukee or Cleveland when lead singer Wendy O. Williams was arrested on obscenity charges. Yet this is nothing new. The Plasmatics have simply brought to the stage what others have sung about and acted out in their "private" lives for years.

Ted Nugent, quoted at the beginning of this chapter, freely admits that his performances are usually accompanied by having sex with one or more groupies. [17] Van Halen's popular album titled *MCMLXXXIV* (1984) features a cut called "Hot for Teacher." Lyrics on Duran Duran's *Rio* album suggest sexual encounters, and their video *Girls on Film* was actually banned in the U.S. and England because of its explicitness. Mail-order record clubs have even begun coding certain albums with a special symbol to warn buyers that the album contains objectionable material.

Added to all of this is an increasing emphasis on sodomy, transvestism, and worse. Boy George of Culture Club is only one of the most showy performers to flaunt bisexual tendencies. Lou Reed, David Bowie, Iggy Pop, and Elton John have done the same. Other groups like the Village People openly advocate homosexuality. Some, like Alice Cooper, even go so far as to exalt necrophilia (an erotic obsession with corpses).

Boy George, like some others, has avoided the question of whether he is really bisexual or is simply seeking publicity. Nevertheless, whether it is a put-on or not, by dressing as a woman he is using sexual perversion for personal gain.

Pizza or Poison?

We've looked at the lives of a number of popular

groups and performers. However, our tour was not comprehensive, so if your favorite wasn't mentioned don't assume all is well! [18] This chapter only touches on the worst excesses and cannot be used as a "catalog" to find which groups are acceptable and which are not.

God calls on the Christian to "flee also youthful lusts: but follow righteousness, faith, charity, peace, with them that call on the Lord out of a pure heart." [19] Does the lifestyle of the typical rock star demonstrate these qualities? No. Are these performers good models— in behavior, in taste, even in their dress—for the young person to follow? Again, the answer according to scriptural standards must be no.

God tells the Christian to avoid even the appearance of evil. [20] Can you do that while actively involved in the rock culture? Think about our analogy. Even if your favorite performer's life is nearly perfect and his or her music seems good, how will you find the "good" without sorting through the garbage that surrounds it? Won't you be heard or seen by others while "sorting"—if you listen to rock or watch MTV? Is that avoiding the *appearance* of evil? Is there a chance that the person who sees you may think that you endorse *all* of what you are hearing?

These are serious questions for Christians who want to dabble with rock. Even more serious issues will be raised in the next two chapters. Meanwhile, what will you have—pizza or poison?

Endnotes

1. Charles M. Young, "Ted Nugent's Bloodlust Rock," *Rolling Stone* (August 25, 1977), 11-13.

2. I Corinthians 2:12-16.

3. Philippians 4:13.

4. Romans 6:1-2.

5. Charles M. Young, "Ted Nugent's Bloodlust Rock," *Rolling Stone* (August 25, 1977), 11-13.

6. Patrick Anderson, *The Milwaukee Journal Magazine* (October 12, 1975), 43.

7. Charles M. Young, "Ted Nugent's Bloodlust Rock," *Rolling Stone* (August 25, 1977), 13.

8. Tim Schnecklot, "Frank Zappa: Garni du jour, Lizard King Poetry and Slime," *Downbeat* (May 18, 1978), 17.

9. See the article on the Maharishi in *Current Biography Yearbook 1972* (New York: H. W. Wilson Co., 1973), pp. 300-303.

10. David Felton, "The Healing of Brother Bri," *Rolling Stone* (November 4, 1976), 36.

11. "Indecent Expenses," *New York* (February 13, 1984), 30.

12. Ibid.

13. Albert Goldman, *Elvis* (New York: McGraw-Hill Book Company, 1981), p. 23.

14. "Indecent Expenses," *New York* (February 13, 1984), 35.

15. For readers not involved in rock, a "groupie" is a female fan who seeks out members of a rock group—backstage, in their hotel, or wherever group members congregate—for the purpose of meeting them on a more personal basis than simply attending their concert. Frequently, sexual favors are traded for the opportunity to spend time with the performers.

16. Ephesians 5:18.

17. Charles M. Young, "Ted Nugent's Bloodlust Rock," *Rolling Stone* (August 25, 1977), 11-13.

18. Readers who would like more information about various groups should consult one of the sources listed in the Appendix entitled "Additional Reading" at the back of this book.

19. II Timothy 2:22.

20. I Thessalonians 5:22.

How Did the Devil Get Involved?

4

Be sober, be vigilant; because your adversary the devil, as a roaring lion, walketh about, seeking whom he may devour: Whom resist stedfast in the faith.
—I Peter 5:8-9a

The Devil's Music?

Musical trends *are* sometimes criticized before they are understood. For example, consider this criticism:

> Music was originally discreet, seemly simple, masculine, and of good morals. Have not the moderns rendered it lascivious beyond measure?

That sounds as though it could have been said about rock. But it was written before the time of Bach, Beethoven, and Brahms![1]

As a result, when young people today hear rock described as "the devil's music," there is a natural tendency to think that these criticisms are nothing more than history repeating itself. "After all," they say, "this is really just a matter of taste. If only my parents (pastor, teacher, etc.) were my age, they would be listening to exactly the same music."

If we were only talking about musical structure or form (the melodic, harmonic, and rhythmic components of rock), that might be so. But the issues are larger than that. We are not simply talking about taste. Satan has gotten a real foothold in rock. That means that we have to be prepared to answer the questions, "How did the devil get involved—and why?" More important, after we see Satan's influence on contemporary music, we must answer a third question: "As a Christian, what should my response be?"

Understand That the Devil Is Real

When Peter wrote that the devil is seeking to devour us, the Holy Spirit led him to use an interesting Greek word for "devour." Literally, it means to "drink down" or to "swallow up whole." In short, if you take a casual approach to Satan (as many popular rock groups do), you aren't just making a lunchtime choice between pizza or food poisoning. You are about to *become* lunch—for the devil!

Some who call themselves Christians have the notion that the devil doesn't really exist. Don't fool yourself. The Bible says that he is real. It even describes the encounter Christ had with Satan during our Lord's earthly ministry. [2]

If Satan is so bold that he would try to swallow up Christ, you can be sure he will try no less with you or with me. The Christian should thank God that "greater is he that is in you, than he that is in the world." [3]

Why Satan Uses Rock

In chapter two, we saw evidence of Satan's influence. Rock has become a stronghold for violence, false religion, drug use, and sexual sin. Whenever possible, Satan will use this dark side of rock to lead Christians into sin.

Even if the Christian does not fall into open sin, rock's effects are still useful to the devil. For example, Satan can sometimes get Christian young people to snicker at the sexual references in a song or a musicvideo. When Satan has done this, he has taken away any testimony that person can have for Christ.

You see, you often become a more effective tool of Satan if you *don't* participate in gross sins. Instead, you simply become an imitation Christian—going through the motions of religion. Your service for God is ended. At the same time, you confuse others who look to you as an example of what a Christian should be. As long as they don't realize they are only looking at a shell, Satan has accomplished his purpose.

But Satan's objective isn't only to promote sin and confusion. He wants *worship*—just as he did when he was cast out of heaven by God. [4] Notice that Satan's desire didn't change, even when he tried to tempt Christ. What did he say? "All these things will I give thee, if thou wilt fall down and worship me." [5]

Since Satan seeks the same thing today, Christians would be foolish to think that he would not try to use a device as powerful as rock for his purposes. Satan will always use the most effective methods that he can; so, since rock appeals to millions, he will use it to great advantage. Satan wants worship, and that is exactly what he is receiving today through the medium of rock.

In Satan's Service

KISS—what does it mean? It depends on whom you ask, but almost anyone who has followed rock during the past several years can tell you that the letters stand for either *K*nights, *K*ings, or *K*ids *I*n *S*atan's *S*ervice.

This group's dabbling in satanism has been ludicrous and silly for the most part. Much of KISS's "evil" seems to be nothing more than record industry hype designed to keep the group in the public eye. Their original theatrical makeup and costumes, the stories of blood from their veins being mixed with ink to print a comic about the group, and their television cartoons have all helped create an all-too-casual, fairy-tale feeling about their image.

KISS has now fallen from the charts and dropped their makeup. The band now performs in far smaller arenas than their concerts once filled. Nevertheless, KISS is no laughing matter. Any group that plays with satanism, whether as a put-on or not, is on the most dangerous ground imaginable.

Black, Blacker, and Blackest

Group names, along with album and song titles, tell us a lot about the focus of rock's attention. Consider the popular group of the seventies, Black Sabbath. A survey of the group's albums reveals one called *We Sold Our Soul for Rock 'n' Roll* and another titled *Live Evil.* Song titles include "Lord of This World," "Children of the Grave," "The Wizard," "Voodoo," and "Heaven and Hell." Black Sabbath has also served as a springboard for the careers of popular solo performers Ozzy Osborne and Ronnie James Dio (formerly of Rainbow), both known for violent or satanic records and musicvideos. Not surprisingly, Osborne, like Stevie Nicks (the ex-lead singer for Fleetwood Mac), has voiced an open interest in witchcraft.

Black Oak Arkansas is another group that has capitalized on a satanic image. Album titles like *Keep the Faith, Raunch and Roll,* and *Race with the Devil* provide some idea about their message. Jim Dandy Mangrum is pictured on a cross on one of the group's albums. "The Day Electricity Came to Arkansas" is also said to be one of many rock songs to contain subliminal messages hidden by a studio technique called "back masking" or "backward masking." (See the Appendix for a discussion of this concept.)

The group AC/DC adds titles like *Highway to Hell, Dirty Deeds Done Dirt Cheap,* and *Back in Black.* The term *AC/DC* was used as a slang term for bisexuals long before this group adopted it. The lightninglike-slash logo that the group uses between the two pairs of letters is also interpreted by some as a satanic S, similar to the shape of the letters used by KISS.

Satanic references may not always be so apparent. A classic example was released by one of the most popular groups of the late 1970s, The Eagles. In the song "Hotel California," the hotel is called a "lovely" place—but a place where you check in and can never check out! Founder of the Church of Satan, Anton LaVey, is pictured in a window of the hotel on the album jacket.

Numerous other groups flirt with satanism and blasphemy. Without attempting to list all, religious references abound in group names like Genesis, Judas Priest, Nazareth, and Styx (the name of a mythical river in hell). Genesis made their interests clear on an early album that features a song promising that 666 (the number of the Antichrist in Revelation) was no longer alone. And some, like Blue Oyster Cult, take their stand through songs like "Don't Fear the Reaper," encouraging men and women living in sin not to fear the end of their lives.

Many of these groups are immensely popular. Most are active in the new video market. Their emphasis on violence and perversion, along with satanism, only seems to make their fling with the devil more commercially successful. Satan is receiving the attention of an entire generation—while Christ is ignored, blasphemed, and mocked.

The Stones, Pink Floyd, and Led Zeppelin.

A "haunted" mansion, blasphemous psalms, gruesome deaths, and hits like "Sympathy for the Devil" and "Dancing with Mr. D"—are these themes that fans should expect from rock's supergroups? These themes are drawn from the music and lives of three of the most commercially successful groups in the history of rock: Led Zeppelin, Pink Floyd, and The Rolling Stones.

Sympathy for the Devil. The Stones, already mentioned in chapter two, have an especially checkered history. Brian Jones, guitarist and a founder of the group, died mysteriously in his swimming pool. The official cause was reported as "death by misadventure." Jones's interest in voodoo and the occult is reflected in the group's recordings of "Sympathy for the Devil" and "Dancing with Mr. D." Both feature backgrounds reported to be recorded voodoo ceremonies and screams of demon possession.

Keith Richards, another member of the group, has said that he is nothing more than a medium (a medium is a person who claims to be able to communicate with the dead). Their songs, he says, are not written, but simply "received." Richards's common-law wife is also involved with the occult and is even said to have cast a spell resulting in the death of a young man. [6]

Blasphemous Rock. Pink Floyd sells its evil with more subtlety. Formed by four students, "Big Pink" became one of the most commercially successful groups of its type. Its album, *Dark Side of the Moon*, remained on *Billboard* magazine's rock album charts longer than any release before 1980. Its video, *The Wall*, continues to sell well. Roger Waters, who played bass and sang for the group, has gone on to solo video efforts.

Despite their commercial success, little attention has been given to the satanic symbols used by the group. Photos on their album jackets feature spontaneous combustion (flames engulfing a man, a phenomenon associated with witchcraft) and the five-pointed star displayed point downward. Such stars are often used in the Church of Satan's literature.

One album features an especially strange photo of the group's instruments carefully arranged in the roadway in front of their van. Only after studying the photo do you realize that their arrangement of the equipment takes the shape of the downward-pointing star that represents the satanic "goathead"—with tympani for eyes and even a "bearded" chin.

The significance of the symbolism on their album jackets is confirmed by the group's blasphemous rendering of the twenty-third Psalm. On the album titled *Animals,* in the cut called "Sheep," the listener is told that the group has looked across Jordan—but has found that things are not what they seem! The Christian's home in heaven is often pictured as being "over the Jordan." But what does Pink Floyd see? Not the home that the Christian expects! Instead, the song pictures Christians as gullible sheep being led to slaughter by a cruel and merciless god. The song finishes with the promise that, in time, man will resist such slaughter and will even rise up to dethrone God Himself! Pink Floyd's message is clear. So is the Christian's responsibility to shun such evil.

A Stairway to Heaven? Did Led Zeppelin sing about a "Stairway to Heaven" or a highway to hell? That title, from one of their most popular songs, hardly disguises the interests pursued by the group. Lead singer Robert Plant and guitarist Jimmy Page have made no effort to

40

conceal their fascination with the occult. Page has run an occult bookstore and even purchased the mansion of the late satanist Aleister Crowley—a site where human sacrifices are reported to have taken place while Crowley was alive.

Deaths and accidents associated with this group only add to its dark reputation. The 1970s brought car crashes and the death of Plant's five-year-old son while the group was touring, followed by the 1980 death of drummer John Bonham in the Crowley mansion. Even writers sympathetic to the group acknowledge that the group has had "a peculiarly tragic record." [7]

Psalm 37 says, "The steps of a good man are ordered by the Lord . . . but the transgressors shall be destroyed together." [8] As the Christian looks at The Rolling Stones, Pink Floyd, and Led Zeppelin, it is difficult not to see the evidence of God's hand against these groups—even now. "The arms of the wicked shall be broken. . . . the seed of the wicked shall be cut off." [9]

The Christian's Response

What should be the Christian's response to Satan's involvement in contemporary music? Paul, writing under the inspiration of the Holy Spirit, makes it clear that this world is a spiritual battleground:

> We wrestle not against flesh and blood, but against principalities, against powers, against the rulers of the darkness of this world, against spiritual wickedness in high places. [10]

If we are involved in a battle, there is a clear necessity to choose a side. The Bible leaves no doubt concerning God's attitude toward witchcraft, wizardry, satanism, and the occult. Deuteronomy 18 says:

> When thou art come into the land which the Lord thy God giveth thee, thou shalt not learn to do after

the abominations of those nations. There shall not be found among you any one . . . that useth divination, or an observer of times, or an enchanter, or a witch, or a charmer, or a consulter with familiar spirits, or a wizard, or a necromancer. For all that do these things are an abomination unto the Lord. [11]

The land spoken of in Deuteronomy was literally the land promised to Israel. However, it is also a picture—a biblical type—of the Christian's salvation. And the Christian is to avoid anything that would give Satan a foothold in his or her life. We must see this danger and then follow the instruction of Proverbs: "Avoid it, pass not by it, turn from it, and pass away." [12]

Endnotes

1. Jacob of Leige, ca. A.D. 1425.

2. Matthew 4:1-11.

3. I John 4:4b.

4. Isaiah 14:12-16.

5. Matthew 4:9.

6. Bob Beeman, *Hear No Evil*, cassette tape.

7. Gary Herman, *Rock 'n' Roll Babylon* (New York: G. P. Putnam's Sons, 1982), p. 161.

8. Psalm 37:23a, 38a.

9. Psalm 37:17a, 28b.

10. Ephesians 6:12.

11. Deuteronomy 18:9-12a.

12. Proverbs 4:15.

Have You Seen the New Songs?

5

You're dealing with a culture of TV babies. What kids can't do today is follow things that are too long. [1]
—MTV executive Bob Pittman

MTV. Some call it a round-the-clock pacifier for TV babies. Others say it's pornography of the worst kind—linking sex *and* violence. Record industry executives are thrilled with its commercial appeal. And the U.S. surgeon general has warned that MTV may be hazardous to your health! [2]

What Is MTV?

MTV is *Music Television*, twenty-four-hour programming of rock music on TV. MTV is actually the "brand name" for a specific cable TV channel operated since 1981 by Warner Communications. However, MTV's popularity spread so quickly, this trademark is sometimes used in a general sense to refer to all TV rock.

Other cable and network channels often broadcast the same content. In your area, these MTV look-alikes may be listed as "Night Tracks" or "Night Flight." Network and local stations may show as little as an hour or so per week, often late Friday or Saturday night. But the success of MTV makes it almost certain that TV rock programming will spread. Estimates published by the National Coalition on Television Violence (NCTV) indicate that there may be as many as 100 local music-video channels soon.[3] Even the 25-54 year olds have become a prime target of videomakers. VH-1 (Video Hits One) has been launched by the same group that is responsible for MTV, and it plans to capture the middle-of-the-road music fan.

This outreach to older listeners is a new twist for the company that made MTV "more than just a network, but a youth-culture phenomenon." By MTV's own admission, the network thrives on its radical approach. "Our promotions have to reinforce our irreverent image . . . We have to push things to an almost outrageous edge."[4]

For readers not familiar with MTV, the basic unit of programming is called "a video." These videos (also called rock videos and musicvideos) are elaborately produced three- to four-minute film clips featuring a rock music background. Industry estimates put the average production cost at $50,000 per video, although clips by various superstars easily exceed twice that amount.

Early videos were provided at no charge to broadcasters by the record companies. These videos were viewed as an advertisement for their records, and MTV was a nonstop outlet for such commercials. But the videos proved to be more entertaining than the records they advertised, so music television was born.

Videocassettes are now charted by *Billboard* magazine along with hit records. While video sales are still only a small percentage of the music industry's total revenue, some are selling well. *The Making of Michael Jackson's 'Thriller'* has reportedly sold over 800,000 copies. In *Thriller* Michael becomes a werewolf and terrorizes his girlfriend. Michael, a member of the Jehovah's Witness cult, disclaims belief in the occult at the start of the video. But despite Michael's disclaimer, the NCTV maintains that the content places it among the most objectionable musicvideos evaluated.

Typical videocassette prices of thirty dollars for an hour-long tape have hampered sales. However, releases of fifteen to twenty minutes are often priced at half that amount, and prices are dropping fast. If this trend continues, young people will soon be asking for their own videocassette playback units rather than stereos and TV's.

Sex, Violence, and More

If it's a *video*, what do they do in front of the cameras? While a few early tapes offered little more than a musical performance, Michael's werewolf is tame stuff beside some of the other videos. A sampling of current offerings includes fist fights, kidnapping, bondage and torture, knives, straightjackets, padded cells, barbed wire, women in cages, nudity, sadism, gangland executions, suggested rape, and war.

A one-year monitoring project by the NCTV yielded the following partial summary of rock on TV:

> Examples of . . . violent musicvideos include *Dynamite* by Jermaine Jackson in which Jermaine and the other men break out of prison only to be chased down by sadistic women jailers; *I Can't Drive 55* by Sammy Hagar where Sammy fights police when arrested for speeding . . . Sammy and his band brawl with police and judge in the courtroom; *Looks That Kill* by Motley Crue with women in cages kept by the Crue and freed by a laser-shooting woman ... *Torture* by Michael Jackson in which sadistic women whip skeletons; *The Last in Line* by Ronnie Dio

where a young delivery boy is caught and taken into a monster world with human captives . . . human beings are sadistically electrocuted by Ronnie Dio when they lose video games.

I Wanna Rock by Twisted Sister has a teacher trying to blow up Twisted Sister. *We're Not Going to Take It* has the same teacher-father hollering at his son who joins Twisted Sister in repeatedly slamming a door on the father. He gets blasted out the window by Twisted Sister music. This later video has been named as causing one imitation [similar] murder in New Mexico . . . *Rock High School* by Heaven shows rock stars throwing away their books and battling a sadistic principal and high school guards armed with shotguns and dobermans . . . . [5]

Women, along with authority figures like fathers, teachers, principals, police, and judges, are fair game for video violence. Mocking religion is also typical. One video by The Night Rangers centers on graduation from a Catholic girls' school. As the graduates leave, they are seen shedding both their graduation robes and their inhibitions. Videomakers, of course, see no distinction between Bible-based Christianity and Roman Catholicism or cults like Jackson's Jehovah's Witnesses. Almost all religion becomes a target for mockery.

The video trend also sends fans to the movies more often. Films like *Flashdance, Footloose,* and *Purple Rain* are little more than extended videos. *Footloose,* like a number of TV videos, also slaps at religion by setting the kids at odds with their parents and a preacher who opposes having a high school graduation dance.

Rock videos have even replaced disco in some nightclubs. The Schaumburg Snuggery, northwest of Chicago, features eleven large screens and a staff of "veejays" (video jockeys) to play the tapes. As *Time* magazine puts it, "the vidblitz" is on! [6]

But Aren't There Some Good Ones?

Like rock records, not all videos deal with sex and violence. Some are created to present what videomakers and the NCTV see as a positive or pro-social message. Examples cited usually include *It's All Right* by Sean Lennon (nine-year-old son of Beatle John Lennon), *Ebony and Ivory* by Paul McCartney and Stevie Wonder, and several releases by the group U-2. U-2 even professes to be a Christian group. However, their message is more nearly a social gospel—demonstrated by their antiwar *New Year Day* and the dedication of their video *Pride* (which is about Christ) to Martin Luther King, Jr.

Also like contemporary records, the professionalism of these productions is becoming very high. Madonna's video, *Like a Virgin*, was filmed in Venice at a cost of $150,000. Top producers and film/videotape editors are also involved. Producer Bob Giraldi only works with top attractions like Diana Ross and Paul McCartney. Don Wilson, who reportedly edited sixty-five videos last year, also edited the 1984 summer Olympic TV coverage for ABC. [7]

Why Should We Be Concerned?

The *content* of most rock videos should be enough cause for alarm. MTV provides a graphic look at what rock stars think. Parents, teachers, and pastors have been told by rock fans, "Aw, that's not what the lyrics mean." Music television is a visualization on film of *exactly* what the performers are thinking and are wanting the listener to think. Musicvideo's window into the world of rock confirms the stories of sexual perversion and violence that have been reported for years.

However, the *concept* of these videos also worries

Christians and others who are concerned about the stability of our society. Rock videos connect sex with violence in a way that some observers think will keep young people from having normal relationships with the opposite sex. Surgeon General C. Everett Koop explains, "The pornographic part of the world says the myth of life is women want to be raped and the violent part says that men want to do it." [8] MTV panders to this image of contemporary society, often making women nothing more than the object of a man's lustful desires.

Dr. Thomas Radecki, of the NCTV, is also a psychiatrist associated with the University of Illinois School of Medicine. He adds, "The violent images of many heavy metal groups . . . portray a worship of violence that I find affecting a number of young people in my psychiatric practice. Young boys and girls come in my office wearing metal-studded jewelry, barbed-wire necklaces, and T-shirts portraying gruesome and evil violence. These same patients have all had problems with serious anti-social behavior." [9]

The MTV executive quoted at the beginning of this chapter points out how industry executives see young people: TV babies having a very limited span of attention. Rock videos are viewed by the industry as the ultimate musical babyfood—packaged in easy-to-swallow, three-minute spoonfuls and available twenty-four hours a day. But you don't need to watch video rock to get a daily dose of its effects. Product ads ranging from jeans to automobiles are being influenced by rock video production techniques. Surrealistic settings—dream-like, often at night, with the action partially obscured by mist or smoke—frequently owe their inspiration to musicvideos. And why not? Many of the same directors and technicians are producing both.

In addition to the videos themselves and their effects on advertising, network TV shows have begun to imitate MTV. "Miami Vice" is the first of a new kind of programming, described as "cop show meets music-video."[10] A feature article that reviewed "Miami Vice" in *New York* magazine pointed out that "the sound-track—Cyndi Lauper, the Pointer Sisters, Lionel Richie, the Stones—bullies us into knowing how to feel. . . . Does this sound like an hour-long video? Well, it looks like one, too. (It *will* be one soon, and a soundtrack will be released . . . by MCA.)"[11]

Even contemporary Christian performers have flocked to the video. We'll return to the CCM videos in chapter seven, but this trend is a good indication of the widespread effect MTV and its look-alikes are having on our society.

Should a Christian Watch MTV?

There is no possible way a young person, controlled by the Holy Spirit and seeking to live for God, can watch video rock. That statement sounds inflexible—and it is. While the old nature might find it exciting, there is often little difference in tuning in MTV and turning the pages of a pornographic magazine. MTV offers less flesh, although a few videos do suggest sexual intercourse (*Adult Education* by Hall and Oates, for example). However, the violence, the influence of the occult, and the bizarre images more than compensate for less nakedness.

If you watch rock video stations, you deliberately subject yourself to strong sexual temptations and ungodly thoughts. "Ye cannot drink the cup of the Lord, and the cup of devils: ye cannot be partakers of the Lord's table, and of the table of devils" (I Corinthians 10:21). This should be a warning to the Christian.

Endnotes

1. Information on musicvideos is scattered. This quotation comes from an article by Lloyd Billingsley that appeared in *Christianity Today* ("Rock Video: 24-hour-a-day Pacifier for 'TV Babies,'" July 13, 1984, 70). You may also want to see "Betting Millions on Four-Minute Musicals," in *Fortune* magazine, September 17, 1984. Rock videos were *Time's* cover theme for December 26, 1983, accompanied by a seven-page article. Numerous local newspapers have also run features, including the *St. Louis Globe Weekend* on April 21, 1984.

2. Surgeon General C. Everett Koop, in an address given at the Medical University of South Carolina reported in the *Greenville Piedmont*, March 16, 1984.

3. From a December 10, 1984, news release published by the National Coalition on Television Violence. This organization monitors rock video programming and publishes an informative newsletter as part of its continuing opposition to televised violence. For more information, write Dr. Thomas Radecki, M.D., National Coalition on Television Violence, P.O. Box 2157, Champaign, IL 61820.

4. Susan Spillman, "Syke-edelic: 'Mr. Excitement' Puttin' on the Hits," *Advertising Age* (January 10, 1985), 4.

5. December 10, 1984, news release published by the National Coalition on Television Violence.

6. *Time* (December 26, 1983), 54.

7. *Fortune* (September 17, 1984), 172-173.

8. *Greenville Piedmont* (March 16, 1984).

9. December 10, 1984, news release published by the National Coalition on Television Violence.

10. John Leonard, "State of the Art: The Cool Heat of 'Miami Vice,'" *New York* (February 25, 1985), 40.

11. Ibid.

Questions, Answers, and Objections

6

Because it is written, Be ye holy; for I am holy.
—I Peter 1:16

In the last three chapters, you've seen some of the problems associated with rock. Contemporary music is a hodgepodge of violence, false religion, sexual immorality, alcohol and drug use, and fascination with the occult. As we saw in chapter four, some groups even go so far as to exalt Satan. Given the information we have about rock, what does the Bible say that we should do?

God's Message Concerning Rock Music

First, we are to *act* on the information we have. God tells us in Isaiah that we are to "cease to do evil" and "learn to do well." [1] Notice that our responsibility is to stop doing any evil thing as soon as we recognize it as evil—an immediate obedience to our Lord's command. The first five chapters of this book have already given you enough information to make the right response to contemporary music.

If we are to act, what shall we do? We are to separate

ourselves *from* sin and *unto* God. In II Corinthians 6:14, Paul asked the Corinthian church, "What fellowship hath righteousness with unrighteousness? And what communion hath light with darkness?" What does the Christian have in common with the rock performers who are fornicators, drug users, and satanists? Nothing, if we are Christ's.

We are not to participate in their sin. That includes financial support through the purchase of records and concert tickets that permit groups to continue in sin. The music industry, like all businesses, responds to consumer preferences. You "vote" with your dollars. When a rock record is purchased, profits are channeled back to the record companies. Print and mechanical royalties are funneled back to the group and the group's publishing company. Concert income encourages the increasingly bizarre performances and elaborate staging that have characterized rock tours over the past several years. You become a direct means of supporting these groups' philosophies and sin. Yet the Bible's instruction is clear: "Come out from among them, and be ye separate, saith the Lord." [2] *Personal separation from sin is not an option.* It is a Bible command. "Be not conformed to this world." [3]

At the same time, we should realize that gaining spiritual maturity and a better understanding of God's will takes time—we are to *learn to do well.* "Learning to do well" means that, if you have been a rock fan, you are going to have to devote as much time to replacing this music as you did to enjoying it. It won't be a quick or an easy task.

This chapter answers a number of the most common objections that are offered by young people who are challenged to give up rock. And it closes with a brief discussion of the real issue: are we willing to forsake rock and pursue personal holiness to follow Christ, or will we turn back to the world?

Guilty by Association

Many Christians agree that *participation* in the sins that are flaunted in the music and lifestyle of rock musicians cannot be tolerated. Yet we often fail to realize that *association* with them is just as serious. We act as though we can feed from the garbage but avoid food poisoning.

The Bible tells us that we are to avoid even the *appearance* of evil. [4] This is the problem with what some call the "good" songs—others use the term *soft rock*—and the songs without words. First, we cannot find them without sorting through the sin. No one publishes a "sanitized" Hot 100 for Christians. Even if there were such a chart, where would money spent on "good" records be going? Right back to the record companies that support and encourage the sin described in the last two chapters!

Beyond that, the Christian must avoid anything that is a hindrance to other Christians. The strong Christian is told to bear the infirmities of the weak and not to insist on his own "rights." [5] What would a new Christian, or a spiritually immature Christian, think if he visited your home and heard what sounds like the music he may have just given up when he was saved? Should he conclude it's all right, after all? How will you explain that you listen to "only the good songs"? "Let not . . . your good be evil spoken of . . . for he that in these things serveth Christ is acceptable to God." [6]

Arguments and Objections

When the Lord began to convict me about my musical standards, my first reaction was to look for reasons why I should stay involved in rock. At the time, I thought they were good reasons. I even thought they were *original* reasons—the product of deep thought about the matter of rock and Christianity. I have since found that almost everyone who is faced with giving up contemporary music offers many of the same reasons why it shouldn't really be necessary to make a total break with rock.

As a result, perhaps it would be helpful to discuss some of the most common arguments and objections raised by rock fans. If you recognize any of your arguments here, pay particularly close attention to the Bible's answers. If, on the other hand, you are trying to help someone who is involved with rock, this section should prepare you for at least some of the objections you are likely to face.

It's All an Image

Those who offer this argument want to believe that statements made by popular performers are just hype— exaggerations designed to make them appear more outrageous for the purpose of generating publicity. Similar statements have been made more recently by MTV executives about violent, sexually explicit videos. These videos are just "spoofing," they say. [7]

This argument simply is not credible. It does not stand up to the available evidence. Live performances, along with reports by those who have traveled with these groups and books published by insiders who have actually lived with major performers, confirm that the debauchery and sin is more than hype.

The Bible says that this is exactly what the Christian should expect from the lives of these performers. God says, "As [a man] thinketh in his heart, so is he" and, "Every good tree bringeth forth good fruit; but a corrupt tree bringeth forth evil fruit." [8] The statements and actions of these performers are not hype. They are the products of their unregenerate hearts. We are also told that "out of the abundance of the heart the mouth speaketh. A good man out of the good treasure of the heart bringeth forth good things: and an evil man . . . bringeth forth evil things." [9]

Finally, even if the statements and actions of popular performers were only hype, by making statements or suggesting actions contrary to God's Word, they are mocking God. If you identify yourself with such performers by listening to their records, by wearing T-shirts that feature their names or the group's logo, or by attending their concerts, *you* are mocking God. Even kidding about this group or that group is a sin. "Every idle word that men shall speak, they shall give account thereof in the day of judgment." [10] We are not to joke about that which is contrary to God's will. We are to be "careful to maintain good works" rather than carelessly making light of sin. [11]

Our Perspective Changes

This objection is offered by young people who observe that music that was once regarded as wrong is sometimes accepted later—or enthusiastically embraced by those who originally opposed it. After all, they say, many of the adults who condemned Elvis in the 1950s became his biggest fans ten to twenty years later.

But God's standards are absolute and unchanging. We're told that "all Scripture is given by inspiration of God." [12] The Bible's teachings are not subject to revision. When rock performers flaunt God's commands, they sin. It doesn't matter whether the one singing is Elvis or Prince.

Christians are not to drift away from the Bible's teachings just because ten years have passed, or twenty years have passed, or *one hundred* years have passed. If sex outside marriage was wrong when the Bible was written, it is wrong now. If sodomy (homosexuality) was wrong when the Bible was written, it is wrong now. And if incest was wrong when the Bible was written, then it is still wrong now—regardless of whether Prince sings "Sister, Sister" and thousands of people buy the record. When we depart from Bible standards, we are no different than the people to whom God sent Jeremiah. They were told, "Stand ye in the ways, and see, and ask for the old paths." But they said, "We will not walk therein." [13] God's perspective hadn't changed, but theirs had.

Some readers will ask, "Then what about the classical composers who lived in sin? How can we associate ourselves with their music, knowing that they lived immoral lives, too?" First, many did *not* live in sin. In fact, there is good evidence that some of the finest composers of past centuries were Christians. Bach is probably the best example.

Second, even those composers who lived immoral lives generally did so privately. The music itself does not suggest sin, unlike so much of today's music. Also, the composers themselves are not alive today, giving interviews and exalting sin through their personal lives. In that respect, quite a contrast exists between Wagner, for example, and Mick Jagger of The Rolling Stones.

Third, the fact that music has survived from centuries past shows that such music has some intrinsic merit—some worth—beyond its popular appeal at the time it was written. To a certain extent, such works become disassociated with the composer and take their place in the historical and developmental flow of western music. Of course, if a Christian listener is aware of some sinful association with a specific piece of music, he or she will want to shun that music as a matter of conscience before the Lord.

I Don't Listen to the Lyrics

Whether you listen to the lyrics or not, there is still the problem of association with sin. That is sufficient reason for the Christian to give up rock. But even beyond that, you should be aware that your mind continuously takes in information—without your conscious awareness. This ability of our minds is called "subliminal perception."

"Subliminal" refers to something done so that its effects are below the level of consciousness. "Perception," of course, is simply our ability to perceive—to receive information. Experiments with a tachistoscope proved that our minds can receive information without our conscious awareness. The tachistoscope, which works something like a high-speed slide projector, was used to flash a message on the screen in motion picture theaters. Viewers were not aware that they were being shown messages that were designed to convince them to buy popcorn or soft drinks. However, the messages worked! During one six-week test, popcorn sales increased by almost sixty percent and drink sales by about twenty percent.

If our minds are capable of this kind of unconscious retention of information, we have a responsibility to be careful about what we take in. "Know ye not that ye are the temple of God, and that the Spirit of God dwelleth in you? If any man defile the temple of God, him shall God destroy." [14]

The Loudness/Beat Has No Effect on Me

This book has said little about the popular theories that the loudness, the beat, or both may have physical and emotional effects. However, if we are subjected to extremely loud sound of any kind—whether it's the blast from a jet aircraft engine or the sound of amplified musical instruments—we endanger our hearing. That's a medical fact, having nothing to do with theories suggested by critics of rock music.

The sound level at many concerts is beyond the level at which your hearing can be damaged. Moreover, if you actually play in a band, depending on the arrangement of the stage and amplification equipment, you may be subject to even higher levels of sound.

Without speculating about other ways music affects us, it is interesting to note that even those who argue *in favor of* rock admit *something* happens when the band begins to play. Steve Lawhead, in a book published by InterVarsity Press, suggests that Christians should give rock another chance. In part, he makes this argument because he feels the Christian is strong enough to resist any effects rock may have. He also argues that the music itself has no effect (i.e., the loudness and the beat do not exert a subconscious influence). For example, he makes the statement, "All music affects people emotionally but *does not* short-circuit the normal mental processes." [15]

Less than forty pages later he contradicts himself, saying, "Music can be thought of as pure communication, since *in many ways it seems to bypass the intellect and speak directly to the inner person.*" [16] Even this would-be defender of rock sees the problems with justifying rock on any spiritually *or* logically consistent basis.

It's Just a Matter of Taste

We discussed this in earlier chapters. If we were talking about musical structure or form, the taste argument might hold. But the issues are holiness and obedience to God's Word. Christians are told in Galatians 1:4 that Christ gave Himself "that he might deliver us from this present evil world." But instead of praising God for this deliverance, too many Christian young people attempt to cling to the world's music.

Often, when the issue of taste is raised, rock fans will also argue that the music is really amoral. The frequency, the amplitude, and the other characteristics of sound are "neutral." Therefore, combining them in a different way than previous generations is simply a question of musical preferences, and not a question of good and bad.

As we'll discuss again in chapter nine, when music is reduced to its smallest component parts, the building blocks themselves are amoral. There is nothing inherently evil about a 440 Hz pitch or a dotted quarter note followed by an eighth note. The same could be said for a drop of paint, or a letter of the alphabet, or a particle of clay. But as soon as a human being combines any of these "building blocks," the creative process has begun and the resulting creation always reflects the view of life held by its composer or artist.

As a result, the Christian is brought back to I Thessalonians 5:22. We must "abstain from all appearance of evil." While music in its smallest component parts may be amoral, and while certain songs (particularly those without words) may be unobjectionable, Christians blur the distinction "between the holy and profane" and "between the unclean and the clean" when they identify themselves with contemporary music. [17] Listening to rock is not just a matter of taste. It is a matter of association with the evil already discussed in earlier chapters.

To Suppress Rock Is Censorship

There are those who feel that the act of establishing musical standards constitutes censorship—particularly if these standards are enforced. Christian parents, churches, and schools that take a stand against rock are labeled antiquated, authoritarian, and repressive.

Societies that endure always censor according to their goals. [18] That which conflicts with their goals is either rejected or labeled as potentially dangerous. Subgroups within the society—homes, schools, churches, and organizations—do the same.

The Bible teaches us that we are to "prove all things; hold fast that which is good." [19] We are also told

Whatsoever things are true, whatsoever things are honest, whatsoever things are just, whatsoever things are pure, whatsoever things are lovely, whatsoever things are of good report; if there be any virtue, and if there be any praise, think on these things. [20]

Clearly, the Bible teaches censorship. We are to censor, or select, those things that are acceptable to God. We are to reject that which is carnal and worldly. In this way, Christians become spiritually mature, one of "those who by reason of use have their senses exercised to discern both good and evil." [21]

I'm Strong Enough

Some Christians actually believe that they are strong enough to withstand the assaults of Satan in rock music. The Bible warns, "Let him that thinketh he standeth take heed lest he fall." [22]

Others believe that they should have the right to listen to rock as a matter of Christian liberty. Obviously, such a person starts by thinking he or she is "strong enough" to listen to this music. But beyond that, the person who listens to rock as a matter of Christian liberty also assumes that *other* Christians will not be affected by this music, causing them to sin.

For this reason Paul, writing under the inspiration of the Holy Spirit, puts real limits on our Christian liberty. You should read all of Romans 14:1-15:1 and I Corinthians 8:1-13. However, the conclusions that Paul makes are expressed in the final verses of each of those sections:

We then that are strong ought to bear the infirmities of the weak, and not to please ourselves. [23]
Wherefore, if meat [rock] make my brother to offend, I will eat no flesh [listen to no rock] while the world standeth, lest I make my brother to offend. [24]

Some wrongly take "offend" to mean "be offended." Reading the verse in that way, they then argue that this makes the strong Christian limited by whatever "foolish" notions the weakest Christian may have. In other words, some say, if rock makes my brother *be offended*, then I will listen to no rock while the world stands. And if he is offended by red socks, I'll wear no red socks—and so on.

That is not the Bible's teaching. "Offend" in I Corinthians 8:13 means to offend *against God*. The proper application of the verse is this: rock contains elements that offend God. If your listening causes another person to listen (and therefore, to offend God), you have sinned. It has little to do with whether you have offended another Christian. The focus is whether you have caused another Christian to sin against God.

In practice, however, Romans 15:1 suggests that we should go one step further and "bear the infirmities of the weak, and not to please ourselves." Does it show Christian love to insist on your "rights," even when you know that a practice is offensive to another Christian? The Bible answers no. "All things are lawful for me, but all things are not expedient." [25]

Rock is not "lawful." Its objectionable elements and worldly associations put it off limits for the Christian— strong or not. But we are on even more dangerous ground when we assume that, in our "strength," we can listen and not cause others to sin by following our example.

Rock Is an Important Barometer of Our Culture

Without question, rock is a mirror of our culture. However, the Christian's position is fixed. His standard is the Bible. Therefore, the need to observe and follow every cultural wind of change is unnecessary. Beyond that, we have many other sources of information about trends in our society.

We are told in Ephesians, "Be no more children, tossed to and fro, and carried about with every wind of doctrine." [26] While the Christian needs to be aware of current trends to know at which points the Christian message is most needed, we have no biblical basis to participate in evil on the grounds that we need to understand it. In this respect, we should heed the words of Paul to the Romans, "I would have you wise unto that which is good, and simple concerning evil." [27] The Greek word for "simple" that Paul uses is interesting in that it has the connotation of remaining "unmixed" with evil. The Bible does not tell us to be *ignorant*, but it clearly teaches that we are to remain *innocent.*

Following the trends in society does not make it necessary to listen to rock music. Listening to rock is first-hand consumption of the sinful product of contemporary performers, and nowhere does the Bible suggest that we may participate in sin and still please God.

There Are Some Good Messages

There are songs that, if it were possible to evaluate them outside the context of the rock culture, are thoughtfully constructed and expressed. However, we are back to the pizza or food poisoning problem. How are we to locate those songs without subjecting ourselves to hours of the more typical rock?

We cannot go where God has not given us liberty to go, even for the sake of a "good" message. To do so violates His commands and exposes us to spiritual danger—and that is presumptuous. The psalmist prayed, "Keep back thy servant also from presumptuous sins." [28]

"But," you might say, "what about [an album, song, or group] that my friend told me about? I didn't have to listen to the other music to find out about it!" Besides the obvious fact that *someone* (your friend in this case) has to sort through the garbage to find the "good" one (and so expose himself to all the evil of the rest), when you listen to rock on the recommendation of a friend, you have lost your testimony to that friend. Rather than taking a clear stand for Christ and for the holiness that the Bible demands, you've said, "Okay, I do want to be a little bit like the world. Thanks for filtering out the worst stuff. Let me hear this album (song, group, etc.) that you like."

What About "Soft Rock"?

The idea that rock offers some good songs or good messages brings us back to the issue of "soft rock." Soft rock is a term sometimes used by Christian young people to distinguish between heavy-metal and the nicer-sounding contemporary music. While the term is not often used outside the Christian community, let's use it here as a convenient label for everything from Air Supply to Dan Fogelberg, along with softer songs by Lionel Richie, Chicago, and many others.

The problems with softer-sounding songs aren't always as obvious, but they are in some ways more dangerous than the music of the heavy-metal groups. Some of the difficulties for the Christian who wants to listen to soft rock are:

1. The message of the music may not be soft.
2. Soft-rock performers don't often stay soft.
3. By listening to soft rock, an appetite for the contemporary sound is developed that becomes difficult to satisfy.
4. The listener would still have to "sort through the garbage" to find these appealing, softer sounds.

We have discussed the fourth problem in some detail, but let's look more closely at the first three. Olivia Newton-John will serve as an example.

When she released "I Honestly Love You," one of her first hits, she presented the image of a blond, well-scrubbed, attractive Australian young lady. Nothing in her appearance would have distinguished her from the students on many Christian campuses. Certainly she

looked nothing like Wendy Williams and other performers whose dress makes it clear what to expect from
their music.

Nor did the sound of her music warn the listener
of problems. "I Honestly Love You" is also a very soft,
pleasant-sounding record. It begins with a piano introduction, followed by a lush, orchestral accompaniment. Everything suggests that this should be an
acceptable contemporary song. But the lyric presents
a picture of a woman longing for an adulterous
relationship!

For example, at one point she sings about seeing her
lover with his wife, while she is with her husband. She
concludes that they will just have to leave the situation
as it is, but she finishes by singing about how much she
still loves him. Although the song leaves open the
question of who is married to whom, if marriage were
not involved, the singer would have been free to date the
person to whom she was singing.

Obviously, the message was not "soft"—not simple
boy-meets-girl music. And Olivia Newton-John's music
did not stay soft. A later album featuring the hit "Let's
Get Physical" was an entirely different sort of music.
In fact, in a radio interview with a successful record
producer who admits liking Olivia Newton-John's
earlier music, he points out that he can no longer play
her albums in his home. Why? He has a five-year-old son
who hears the words and then goes around the house
repeating them![29]

Beyond these problems, the Christian who listens
to soft rock develops an appetite for the contemporary
sound. Even in cases where there is very little wrong
with the music, the desire for that distinct contemporary sound becomes a very difficult habit to break. What
is the "contemporary sound"? No brief description can
cover all of its elements, but two common characteristics are very crisp, clean high frequencies and a very

solid bass. This is in contrast to the predominately mid-range sound of most orchestral recordings.

As a result, the young person who wants to give up rock has a difficult time finding a substitute for this "sound" which has become so satisfying. In my own experience of giving up contemporary music, I found no substitute. The appetite you will develop for the contemporary sound is just one more reason for avoiding even the softer-sounding contemporary groups.

But Christians Are to Be the "Salt"

A number of performers take this approach to their profession of Christianity. Donna Summer, Kerry Livgren (Kansas), and Michael Omartian are examples. However, their willingness to be used by the music industry, while earning large amounts of money *from* it and making large amounts *for* it, does more to compromise the testimony of Christ than to advance His cause. Moreover, while they are part of the rock culture, it is almost inevitable that such performers will adopt at least part of the lifestyle.

Christ did pray to His Father that He should not take Christians out of the world, but that *He should keep them from the evil.* [30] This prayer clearly shows that Christ did not set aside the scriptural teaching that we are to be separate from sin, a holy people for the Lord. Moreover, if we are truly salt, we are to change the world, not permit the world to change us.

What Now?

You may be slow to give up rock, even after seeing its problems. Sometimes this response is the result of a lack of information. However, more often it is because your desire to do God's will is not as strong as your love for rock. The young man described in Matthew 19 had this type of problem, despite his interest in eternal life. In a parallel passage in Mark, the Bible tells us that he even ran to Christ and knelt before Him. But the young man's questions reveal two flaws that kept him from following Christ.

The first is that he wanted to *know* God's will—not necessarily to *do* it, but to see if it fit with his own. He asks Christ, "What shall I do?" And Christ tells him, in effect, "You know the answer, and you knew it even before you asked!" "Thou knowest the commandments." [31]

In effect, the young man was shopping for a "better deal." He was not comfortable with God's will—though he claims to have known the commandments and to have kept them from his youth. If we can believe that he really did know the commandments, undoubtedly the passage that bothered him most is found in Deuteronomy 6:5-6. "Thou shalt love the Lord thy God with all thine heart, and with all thy soul, and with all thy might. And these words, which I command thee this day, shall be in thine heart."

Christ didn't dispute the young man's claim when he said he had kept the commandments. The Lord simply said, "Sell all . . . and come, follow me." [32] With one request, Christ went to the heart of the problem. The young man was having difficulty loving God with *all* his heart and putting Him before his wealth. He had not come to Christ *in total surrender.* He wasn't willing to forsake all. He was hoping there might be an easier answer.

Are you guilty of the same sin? Are you asking God to reveal His will about contemporary music, when you already know the problems?

How Do You See Christ?

The second flaw the passage reveals is that the

young man did not see Christ for who He is. This is demonstrated by his response to Christ's request. Think about it: the Saviour Himself looked at the young man and said, "Come, take up the cross, and follow me." [33] If he had really *believed* Christ was God, don't you think the young man would have done just that?

Christ even reassured him that, whatever he might give up on earth, he would have treasure in heaven. But apparently the young man didn't believe Christ could fulfill that promise. Otherwise, why would he forsake both eternal life and certain treasure? Instead, the Bible tells us that the young man "was sad at that saying, and went away grieved." [34]

What is your response to God's message concerning contemporary music? Are you willing to follow Christ, or are you sad at these sayings—preferring the world instead? As this chapter closes, you have reached a decision point. If you will not see the clear dangers associated with rock, you will not see the more subtle dangers of CCM discussed in section two.

The Bible talks about men and women who will be "lovers of pleasure more than lovers of God." [35] In many ways, that summarizes the story of the young man Christ describes in Matthew 19. What about you? Will you turn back toward the world, or will you be like the believers of whom Paul wrote who "obeyed from the heart that form of doctrine which was delivered [unto them]"? [36] My prayer is that you will be "not unwise," [37] but shall understand what the will of the Lord is about this important issue.

Endnotes

1. Isaiah 1:16b-17a.

2. II Corinthians 6:17.

3. Romans 12:2.

4. I Thessalonians 5:22.

5. Romans 15:1.

6. Romans 14:16, 18.

7. Lloyd Billingsley, "Rock Video: 24 Hour-a-Day Pacifier for TV 'Babies,'" *Christianity Today* (July 13, 1984), 70.

8. Proverbs 23:7; Matthew 7:17.

9. Matthew 12:34-35.

10. Matthew 12:36.

11. Titus 3:8.

12. II Timothy 3:16.

13. Jeremiah 6:16.

14. I Corinthians 3:16-17a.

15. Steve Lawhead, *Rock Reconsidered* (Downers Grove, Illinois: InterVarsity Press, 1981), p. 69.

16. Ibid., p. 105 (italics added).

17. Ezekiel 44:23.

18. For the principles included in this discussion of censorship, I am especially indebted to a lecture by Dr. Ronald A. Horton, Chairman of the Division of English Language and Literature at Bob Jones University.

19. I Thessalonians 5:21.

20. Philippians 4:8.

21. Hebrews 5:14.

22. I Corinthians 10:12.

23. Romans 15:1.

24. I Corinthians 8:13.

25. I Corinthians 10:23.

26. Ephesians 4:14.

27. Romans 16:19b.

28. Psalm 19:13a.

29. Michael Omartian, in an interview titled "Christian Music in the Church and Home," "Focus on the Family" (radio program), 1982.

30. John 17:15.

31. Mark 10:19.

32. Luke 18:22.

33. Mark 10:21.

34. Mark 10:22

35. II Timothy 3:4.

36. Romans 6:17.

37. Ephesians 5:17.

Section Two:
Return of the Giants

If you have ever lived in an area where hurricanes are common, you know that a bad storm can do considerable damage. In fact, an especially bad hurricane can spawn other storms—even tornadoes, which have a life of their own and cause additional destruction.

Many sins are like hurricanes. Their destructive effects are not limited to one smashing blow. Instead, such sins spawn others having a life of their own. These "sons of sin" do additional damage, sometimes reaching areas untouched by the first.

So it was with Goliath. Though slain by David, he had brothers and sons. The Bible tells us that one, called Ishbi-benob, was "girded with a new sword" and would have killed David had not Abishai intervened (II Samuel 21:15–22).

Rock, like Goliath, has sons and brothers. One of these—called Christian rock, contemporary Christian music, or CCM—is girded with a new sword. Fans say it's the sword of the Spirit. "It's the same gospel," they'll tell you, "just set in the language of the times."

Others aren't so sure. There are signs that CCM preaches a new gospel, ignoring basic teachings of the Word of God. Even if this were not so, do we want to use the language of the times when that "language" is tainted with satanism and sin of all kinds?

Chapters seven through nine take a look at CCM. Is this new sound praise for the Most High or simply a musical high for the listeners? We'll look at the music and its message to see if we can find out.

What Is "Christian" Rock?

7

The scene is familiar: a sweating, bearded singer wails onstage amid the din of heavy-metal guitars, synthesizers, and crashing drums.

The lyrics are not: "I used to worship knowledge/ thought it would set me free," screams Glenn Kaiser, lead singer of the band Resurrection. "I found Jesus' love/is quite enough for me. . . ." [1]
—*USA Today*

That description appeared in the national newspaper *USA Today.* The article, by Jack Kelley, describes a weekend "Jesus festival" at the Orlando Fairgrounds that was attended by "15,000 cheering, dancing fans." At the conclusion of one performance, Leon Patillo, formerly of the popular rock band Santana, gave this invitation, "I want you to know this concert ain't nothing but a setup for you. The Lord, man, he's checking you out. You might as well go ahead and be saved."

The music is called contemporary Christian music, or "CCM." Its fans see it as an important weapon in the arsenal of the twentieth-century church. "If we are to evangelize this generation," they say, "we've got to reach young people in their own language." Since most unsaved young people "speak" rock, CCM's logic says draw the kids in with rock and then get them saved with the gospel.

But these would-be soulwinners (CCM'ers generally prefer the term "communicators") aren't the only ones excited about contemporary Christian music. It's one of the hottest items Christian bookstores have seen in years. In some stores it accounts for more than half their total sales.

As you might expect, with this sort of commercial demand an entire industry sprang up to provide a steady stream of CCM releases. Old-timers like Word, Inc., long involved in Christian recordings, haven't missed a beat and now market a complete range of contemporary offerings. Newcomers like Sparrow Records, organized by ex-Word executive Billy Ray Hearn, have become equally powerful forces in the market. Even major labels like CBS, PolyGram, and others have wondered if the gospel might be good for their balance sheets, too.

What Was Wrong with the Music We Had?

CCM fans argue that traditional church music has lost its impact—particularly with young people. Ralph Carmichael was one of the first to voice this argument. Criticized for the new sound of his own music in the early 1970s, Carmichael responds, "The younger generation has been brought up on a different musical diet from their elders, and . . . they speak a different musical language. If you wanted to communicate with people, say, in Greece . . . you would not insist on talking with them in Chinese." [2]

Although Carmichael exaggerates the situation (young people *are* capable of understanding other musical languages), his position has become a battle cry for the CCM movement. One result is that the focus of CCM is on what *works*. Paul Johnson, another early performer of contemporary Christian music, emphasizes this. "The church has embraced a lot of musical change in the last ten years. *It has been forced to because the results have been good.* I would dare say that more people have been drawn to Jesus by Bill Gaither's music . . . than through the sacred music of the Reformation period."[3]

Gaither, of course, has little popularity among younger listeners. The young and musically aware are tuned to other groups with a more contemporary sound. But many pastors agree that CCM works. To quote one pastor, "In addition to the traditional hymns and songs we also try to keep abreast of the times by presenting a considerable amount of the modern music with its contemporary sound. . . . *the name of the game is communication.*"[4]

In just a few years, CCM has spawned a host of enthusiastic defenders. Just a glance at the "Letters to the Editor" columns of most religious magazines shows that CCM's listeners think they've found a good thing. Here is a sampling from one of the magazines most often read by CCM supporters: "I guess there is really hope for Christian music";[5] "Andrae [Crouch] has proven a Jesus-freak can make it in the world without compromising truth";[6] "a lot of churches might not accept [Amy Grant's] new style, but if they're open to God, He will show them";[7] and, finally, "Christians seem to find the worst [look for evil] in everything. U2 is playing to crowds that never heard the gospel."[8] Clearly, these are people who like CCM!

What Is This New Music?

Contemporary Christian music is clearly patterned after rock. Because "rock" has bad associations for some Christians, CCM supporters frequently avoid the word. As a result, labels ranging from "gospel rock" to "Jesus music" are gradually being dropped in favor of the all-inclusive "contemporary Christian music." Usually, "rock" only appears when the record company or performer knows that it will have a positive meaning for young listeners.

However, CCM performers, producers, and fans are quick to point out its similarities to rock. In fact, one book about rock and CCM even finishes with a chart called "Sounds Like . . . ." The chart compares CCM performers to popular rock groups in order to help young people find contemporary Christian music to fit their current tastes. [9]

If CCM's fans define their music in terms of rock, is there any difference? Or is contemporary Christian music no more than a sanitized substitute for rock? To some extent, cleaning up rock's act is part of CCM's purpose. "The words of the songs won't be saturated with references to sex and drugs," says one writer. [10]

But beyond their effort to clean up rock, most CCM performers also express a desire to exalt Christ. It's true, some of these performers are as self-centered and success-oriented as any secular star. Others are rumored as having serious problems with their lifestyle. [11] However, anyone who has listened to a broad cross section of contemporary Christian music knows that some performers genuinely seek to exalt the Saviour. As a result, we must acknowledge this goal in defining CCM. In chapters eight and nine we will evaluate how well it is being accomplished.

Is our picture of contemporary Christian music complete? Not quite. Despite the nominally Christian message of many CCM songs, some performers are now moving in the direction of merely "positive" or life-affirming lyrics. An example is Leon Patillo's popular album, *The Sky's the Limit.* As one reviewer said, "The inspirational title cut expresses the universal theme that we as individuals can do anything when we put our minds to it, because 'the sky is the limit.'" [12]

While other songs by Patillo present a clearer

message, the pressure for commercial success appears to be having an effect. CCM may change a great deal if record companies find that watering down strong Christian content makes CCM acceptable to a larger audience.

Return of the Giants

Contemporary Christian music is a powerful force. The sound has attracted the attention of young and old. Many who are firmly opposed to rock are convinced that we should give CCM a chance.

In chapter eight we'll examine the lifestyle and music of a number of CCM performers. What really attracted the 15,000 fans to the Orlando Fairgrounds? Was it the message of Christ or the music of the world? And if, as CCM fans tell us, rock is a legitimate way to interest young people in the gospel, is anyone getting the message—or have we killed Goliath only to see him replaced by Ishbi-benob?

Endnotes

1. Jack Kelley, "Born-Again Bands' Heavy-Metal Gospel," *USA Today* (June 5, 1984), 5D.

2. Robert A. Cook, "That New Religious Music," *Christian Herald* (December 1976), 7.

3. Paul Johnson, "Is the New Christian Music Too Worldly?," *Christian Life* (May 1976), 25 (italics added).

4. Robert A. Cook, "That New Religious Music," *Christian Herald* (December 1976), 8 (italics added).

5. "Feedback," *Contemporary Christian Magazine* (June 1982), 10.

6. Ibid.

7. "Feedback," *Contemporary Christian Magazine* (May 1984), 6.

8. "Feedback," *Contemporary Christian Magazine* (April 1984), 41.

9. J. Brent Bill, *Rock and Roll: Proceed with Caution* (Old Tappan, New Jersey: Fleming H. Revell Company, 1984), pp. 143-149.

10. Bob Larson, *Rock: For Those Who Listen to the Words and Don't Like What They Hear* (Wheaton, Illinois: Tyndale House Publishers, 1983), p. 95.

11. "Feedback," *Contemporary Christian Magazine* (April 1984), 41.

12. "Music/Records," *Contemporary Christian Magazine* (May 1984), 39.

Does It Look Like a Giant?
8

If we do very many big gigs in a row . . . it's hard for us to go into the small towns and stay in one of those funky hotels they have. At the same time they don't have the type of restaurants that we like to eat at. . . . But fortunately we do all these concerts to keep our ministry humble. [1]
—**Leon Patillo**

The time may come when your town and mine just won't rate a contemporary Christian concert! Meanwhile, Leon and others are still willing to put up with the bad hotels and disappointing restaurants. Of course, concert fees of as much as $20,000 [2] and amenities such as the backstage masseur at a recent Amy Grant concert [3] help ease the pain of performing. But perhaps we can't expect CCM performers to endure these conditions forever.

As we saw in the last chapter, CCM has become a Goliath industry. But in a field where performers use the term "ministry" to describe their careers, what comes first—the money or the ministry?

The Profit Motive: CCM Does Business Like a Giant

It would be difficult not to be tempted by potential profits. "We expect Christian rock to double its selling expectations," says one gospel-industry figure. [4] Even secular executives, such as M. Richard Asher of CBS Records, say, "The religious market has greater potential than rock." [5] The Columbia Record and Tape Club has even begun to list CCM albums alongside those by rock/MTV stars like Lionel Richie. And while Asher may have overstated the case, some performers are doing very well. Amy Grant's successful *Age to Age* album is reported to have sold more than 800,000 copies—far in excess of the 500,000 figure required to qualify as a gold record.

While only a few CCM albums go gold, performers, their publishers, and their labels are prospering. Almost ten years ago, *Billboard* reported "Religious Publishing Flourishing with a Contemporary Emphasis." [6] *Bookstore Journal,* the magazine of the Christian Booksellers Association, reports that Jarrell McCracken of religious conglomerate Word, Inc., has achieved multimillionaire status. [7]

But what effect is this success having on CCM performers and their companies? After all, the Bible promises numerous blessings to the people of God. Perhaps the CCM crowd is only reaping that which has been promised and the critics are motivated more by an attitude of "sour grapes" than by concern for the gospel.

The evidence doesn't support that conclusion. Instead, we see a thriving "industry" which looks more and more like the rock giant. For example, some CCM performers have begun to " 'weed out' [performances in] smaller churches in the name of being 'good stewards' of the artist's time." [8] Smaller churches, of course, are not able to pay the fees that the more popular CCM artists can now command. And *Time* magazine reports that the total sales for the industry exceeded $75 million in 1984. [9]

With this success has come the inevitable touch of Madison Avenue. CCM record ads in publications like *Contemporary Christian Magazine* look very much like their rock cousins in *Billboard*. Record labels seek favorable reviews for their releases—including phrases like "at its rocking best," "simmers down to smooth funk, and cools off in quiet praise," and "an ultra-conservative Christian Black Sabbath." [10] Record ads show no more restraint than the reviews. Word, Inc., shouts, "And you thought Word was crazy last year ... This latest offer is certifiably insane!" [11]

And CCM's bottom line gets the same emphasis it might on Wall Street. Consider the headline of a recent article in *Business Week*, "A Religious Publisher Gets More Worldly About Management." And with yearly sales of $92 million, Zondervan (the company described in this article) has reason to watch its bottom line! [12] In the same year, Sparrow Records, another top label, reported that its sales increased thirty-one percent. [13]

Even the church is invited to get in on a good thing! For between two and three thousand dollars, any church can have a satellite receiving dish installed and throw open its doors to the Church Growth Network (CGN, Inc.). For an affiliation fee plus one dollar admission for each person attending these televised events, Pat Boone and his associates will bring you a complete roster of CCM performers—as CGN's promotions say, "a power-house lineup!"

The Bible tells us that "the laborer is worthy of his [pay]." [14] However, the large incomes, lavish travel and entertainment accounts, and expensive promotions typical of today's CCM industry bear an uncomfortably close resemblance to their secular counterparts.

Worldly Ways: CCM Groups Look Like the Giants

As the "Sounds Like ..." chart mentioned in chapter seven makes clear, not only is CCM rock, but almost all types of rock are available. And these records are professionally produced. If lyrics don't make it clear that you're hearing a CCM hit, the sounds could be right off *Billboard's* pop charts.

This increasing professionalism is a special point of pride to the CCM community. In one sense, it should be. The Bible makes it clear that the Christian should seek to do all things well. However, *affirmation* of high standards is different from the *imitation* of the world.

Sadly, contemporary Christian music is mostly imitation. Since part of CCM's reason for existence is to serve as a sanitized substitute for rock, this lack of originality should be no surprise. But to many CCM performers, the highest possible praise seems to be identification with the secular rock culture. As one article noted, some performers "arduously seek the approval of the secular music world." [15]

Andrae Crouch is a good example. Andrae said of secular rock stars, "We're proud to have them associate with us. It makes us look good, too." [16] Andrae lives what he believes. A year before he made that statement, Crouch appeared on "Saturday Night Live"—a television show often noted for its irreverent and sexually suggestive humor. His personal life has also been the subject of controversy over alleged drug use. [17] Clearly, Andrae has been "successful" in associating himself with the world. The question is whether this association has made him look as good as he had hoped, particularly in light of the Bible's teaching that we are to "abstain from all appearance of evil." [18]

This desire to be identified with the world is not limited to one or two performers. Live concerts and CCM videos reveal striking similarities between secular rockers and many contemporary Christian stars.

Sheila Walsh, a popular CCM attraction, offers a musical style characterized as "streetwise and harsh"—characteristic of less radical punk bands (often called "new wave"). Her act includes "misty fog, shot with brilliantly colored lights . . . [she] moves in robot-like precision. Sparkling fireworks light darkened stage, sometimes crackling along with the bass lines." [19] The similarity to rock videos is no coincidence.

Amy Grant is among the most successful CCM performers. During a St. Louis concert, Amy demonstrated the kind of free-wheeling choreography typical of secular rock before these moves were adopted by CCM. "Amy danced into the spotlight," and followed that entrance with jumps, kicks, and "some blazing air guitar work." According to Amy, "I just decided I know the audience is here to see me and have some fun. So, I'm gonna enjoy myself and not be so concerned about how I look." [20]

CCM fans and performers have eagerly embraced this trend toward flashy visual effects. Musicvideos were a natural follow-up. Bill Hearn, son of the founder of Sparrow Records, reports that two of their recent video productions "have been shown extensively by bookstores and youth groups, as well as Christian and secular independent cable networks. . . . Our road sales organization received repeated requests . . . for commercial products." [21] Performers including Amy Grant, Sheila Walsh, Steve Taylor, Sandi Patti, 2nd Chapter of Acts, and Michael and Stormie Omartian are among the popular CCM performers who are taking advantage of video exposure.

Predictably, many of the same personnel who have their hands in rock videos have also been hired by CCM'ers to do theirs. Steve Taylor's "Meltdown (At Madame Tussaud's)"—a loose satire on the leveling effect of death and judgment—was photographed in the Hollywood Wax Museum by Michael Brown. Editing chores were handled by Millie Paul, who also worked on Michael Jackson's successful video, *The Making of Michael Jackson's 'Thriller.'* The special effects in Taylor's production are by Ken Horn, a Hollywood veteran whose work can be seen in over thirty feature films. [22]

Worldly Wishes: CCM'ers Would Like to Be Among the Giants

Grant is one of CCM's most promising hopes for "crossover"—a term that refers to achieving success in more than one musical market. Crossover, of course, means greater financial success for the performer and for the performer's record label. Amy's label (Word) hired independent promotion men to seek airplay for her records on pop stations. She says, "I'd like to be in the pop mainstream with the music I'm singing, but that may be impossible . . . but I'm still going to keep trying." [23]

Acceptance by the pop mainstream should come easier for Amy than for others. Her goal is entertainment. "I'm a singer, not a preacher . . . I'm not looking to convert anybody." [24] In another interview, she notes, "I want to play hardball in this business. I want to be on the same level professionally with performers in all areas of music. I love to hear Billy Joel, Kenny Loggins and the Doobie Brothers. Why not? I aim to bridge the gap between Christian and pop." [25]

Despite her success, Amy still exercises care not to offend the conservative segments of her market. "I love to dance, but there are people who listen to my music who are uncomfortable with dancing. I have to think of them. I'm not going to say too often that I like a cold beer while watching a football game. That might bother some of my fans too." [26]

Other performers like Kerry Livgren, of the rock group Kansas, and Grammy-winner Donna Summer are already *in* the mainstream. Neither is a strictly Christian performer, in the sense of recording for a CCM label or making most of their record sales in Christian bookstores. However, Livgren writes songs with nominally Christian lyrics. Summer is produced by one of the most talented contemporary Christian performer/producers, Michael Omartian. And the CCM community welcomes Kerry's and Donna's success. As Andrae Crouch said (quoted earlier), "It makes us look good." Presumably he means that the status of these secular stars lends credibility to the CCM movement. Yet, Livgren and Summer are good examples of the spiritual schizophrenia that mixing rock with Christianity can produce.

Both have made professions of faith. Livgren even authored a book describing "his spiritual quest." [27] With gold and platinum albums to the group's credit, Kansas is clearly a commercial success. Did it ever occur to Livgren to come out of the rock culture? Yes, but he explains (in a statement that is hardly original), "Separation does not mean isolation." [28] If he had been a pornography dealer, he admits that it would have been prudent to get out. But simply being *surrounded* by rock's violence and pornography—and luring Christian young people in through his participation—is not reason enough to separate from this evil.

Donna Summer is close to superstar status. Divorced from Austrian actor Helmut Sommer (she kept the name but anglicized the spelling), Donna's early success was in Europe. Her frank sexuality later catapulted her to the top of America's charts. [29] One writer characterized her style as making herself appear available in a "sexually obvious, not to say whorish, way." [30] Yet, the liner notes of one Summer album thank God for His help and end with a paraphrase of John 3:16 and verses from Isaiah 53! [31]

Even if Donna's image was established before she was saved, she has done little to separate herself from it. Worse still, the CCM community's strong craving for commercial success and crossover hits guaranteed her an immediate place among the CCM elite. This overtly success-oriented emphasis and the relative immaturity of many performers has resulted in a "Christian star" system that includes all the marks of worldly fame and success.

CCM Compromise: Religion of the Giant

Aside from its commercialism and its increasing resemblance to the world, contemporary Christian music is becoming a religious melting pot. Some in the community admit that they are not believers.[32] And while this is still an exception, CCM *is proud* of its ecumenical and charismatic spirit. This ecumenism extends open arms toward apostate Protestant denominations and the Roman Catholic Church.[33]

John Michael Talbot notes that after his divorce he thought of giving up his music. Searching for counsel, he visited Alverna—a Franciscan retreat near his parents' home in Indianapolis, Indiana. Eventually, Talbot decided to make his home in this Roman Catholic retreat.

At an appropriate time, John talked with his religious superiors about his music. Talbot entered the CCM movement after leaving the successful secular group, Mason Proffit. His early albums presented a conservative, Protestant theology. He performed often in Bible-preaching (though neo-evangelical) churches. Clearly, John could be useful to the Roman Church.

"Think twice," the priest advised. Aside from the matter of talent, the Franciscan continued, "there is another consideration perhaps just as important, if not more so. You may want to keep in touch with Protestant evangelical Christianity, instead of withdrawing from it. I think God has chosen you as a bridge builder."[34]

The remainder of Talbot's account shows him progressively falling under the spell of Romanist error. He soon concluded that the Protestant Reformation had no basis, and that to deny the authority of the Roman Catholic Church was to deny the church that "gave us the Scriptures." [35] Wholly caught up in the philosophy of his new religion, Talbot was soon received into the Roman Catholic Church.

The charismatic emphasis, though without tongues, is also seen in Talbot's experience. Dreams and other direct "revelations" from God account for his increasing conviction that the Roman Church holds the key to the future. Unhappily, John ignores the biblical teaching that "if they speak not according to this word, it is because there is no light in them." [36] When a dream, an emotional charismatic experience, or a Roman Catholic priest contradicts the Bible, our decision must be made solely on the basis of what the Bible teaches. Paul says it even more strongly in Galatians 1:8. "Though we, or an angel from heaven, preach any other gospel unto you than that which we have preached unto you, let him be accursed."

Other performers add tongues and the "gifts of the spirit," while maintaining Talbot's emphasis on "unity of the body." In fact, "the body" (sadly misused in this context to refer to the Body of Christ) is a favorite term. Typically, only a few minutes' exposure to CCM is needed to catch some of the buzzwords that reflect the ecumenical spirit of CCM—"minister" (as a verb), "anointed" (referring to virtually every performer), "the body" (including almost anyone who claims the label Christian), and "unity" (usually occurring in a context that suggests all doctrinal differences be put aside).

But not all CCM fans live what they preach. Even in this openly ecumenical crowd, fellowship is selective. Singer Sheila Walsh reports being approached by a couple who asked, "Do you believe in the 'Super Nine

All the Time'?" Admitting her ignorance of the meaning of this phrase, Sheila was abandoned by the couple (after they explained that the reference was to gifts of the Holy Spirit that charismatics claim would continue from the day of Pentecost). [37]

Son of David or Son of the Giant?

How do we answer the question posed at the end of the last chapter—what really attracted 15,000 fans to the Orlando Fairgrounds? Was it the message of Christ or the music of the world? The rock sound, the performers' on-stage antics, the Christian star syndrome, and the large financial rewards suggest that fans are attracted by a rocklike musical spectacle rather than the message of Christ.

CCM fans argue that Christ's earthly ministry drew large crowds, too. However, when Christ's mission and His message became clear, it was necessary to ask even His disciples, "Will ye also go away?" [38]

Christians involved with rock—even rock with a vaguely religious message—cease to be a distinct, holy people. When CCM performers look like the world, act like the world, and would enjoy more of the world's success if they could, what remains? "Sanitized" rock is doomed to fail spiritually, if not financially, for the Christian is saved to "walk in newness of life." [39]

Even some CCM fans see the problem. In a letter to *Contemporary Christian Magazine,* one wrote, "If [Amy Grant] hits the pop charts with artists such as Michael Jackson and the Police . . . then I am thought of as one who is a fan of those other artists. I think we can let our light shine without having such a high level of conforming to the other side. If we jump in the sewer, how can we clean anyone up . . . ?" [40]

Can contemporary Christian music live up to its

other goal of reaching young people with the gospel? As we'll see in the next chapter, Scripture makes it clear that CCM has no biblical basis for its ministry until it submits to the clear teachings of God's Word.

Endnotes

1. Carolyn A. Burns, "Settling in with Leon Patillo," *Contemporary Christian Magazine* (June 1982), 14.

2. Richard Dinwiddie, "Moneychangers in the Church: Making the Sounds of Music," *Christianity Today* (June 26, 1981), 17.

3. Bruce Brown, "Ministry Amidst the Fun," *Contemporary Christian Magazine* (May 1984), 35.

4. Jack Kelley, "Born-Again Bands' Heavy-Metal Gospel," *USA Today* (June 5, 1984), 5D.

5. "Music," *Christian Bookseller* (February 1982), 51.

6. "Religious Publishing Flourishing with a Contemporary Emphasis," *Billboard* (March 29, 1975), P-30, P-42.

7. Julie Cave, "Challenged by Change," *Bookstore Journal* (July 1981), 184.

8. Richard Dinwiddie, "Moneychangers in the Church: Making the Sounds of Music," *Christianity Today* (June 26, 1981), 17.

9. Gerald Clarke, "New Lyrics for the Devil's Music," *Time* (March 11, 1985), 60.

10. From a collection of record reviews published between April and June 1984 in *Contemporary Christian Magazine*.

11. *Christian Bookseller* (April 1984), front cover.

12. "A Religious Publisher Gets More Worldly About Management," *Business Week* (June 18, 1984), 92.

13. "Music," *Christian Bookseller* (April 1984), 32.

14. I Timothy 5:18b.

15. Richard Dinwiddie, "Moneychangers in the Church: Making the Sounds of Music," *Christianity Today* (June 26, 1981), 17.

16. Bob Darden, "Contemporary Christian Music: An Overview, Part II," *Christian Bookseller* (February 1982), 62.

17. See "Feedback," *Contemporary Christian Magazine* (April 1984), 41, which comments on an article on Crouch in the February 1983 issue.

18. I Thessalonians 5:22.

19. Carolyn A. Burns, "Sheila Walsh: Radical New Waver or Rebel With a Cause?," *Contemporary Christian Magazine* (May 1984), 27.

20. Bruce Brown, "Ministry Amidst the Fun," *Contemporary Christian Magazine* (May 1984), 35.

21. "Music Video," *Communications for Better Living* (December 1984), 31.

22. Ibid.

23. Dennis Hunt, "Amy Grant: A Phenomenon in Christian Music," in an article copyrighted by the Los Angeles Times, as it appeared in the *Greenville News* (May 4, 1984), 2C.

24. Ibid.

25. Gerald Clarke, "New Lyrics for the Devil's Music," *Time* (March 11, 1985), 60.

26. Dennis Hunt, "Amy Grant: A Phenomenon in Christian Music," in an article copyrighted by the Los Angeles Times, as it appeared in the *Greenville News* (May 4, 1984), 2C.

27. Kenneth Boa and Kerry Livgren, *Seeds of Change* (Westchester, Illinois: Crossway Books, 1983).

28. Ibid., p. 182.

29. John Pareles and Patricia Romanowski, *The Rolling Stone Encyclopedia of Rock and Roll* (New York: Rolling Stone Press/Summit Books, 1983), p. 537.

30. Gary Herman, *Rock 'n' Roll Babylon* (New York: G.P. Putnam's Sons, 1982), p. 83.

31. Donna Summer, *She Works Hard for the Money* (New York: Polygram Records, 1983), album jacket.

32. Richard Dinwiddie, "Moneychangers in the Church: Making the Sounds of Music," *Christianity Today* (June 26, 1981), 16.

33. It is beyond the scope of this book to present a summary course in church history. However, for more information about the growth of unbelief in major Protestant denominations, write *FAITH for the Family* magazine, Greenville, SC 29614. For a very readable and concise summary of the differences between Roman Catholic doctrine and the Bible's teaching, see *Pilgrimage from Rome*, by Bartholomew F. Brewer (Greenville, South Carolina: Bob Jones University Press, 1982).

34. Dan O'Neill, *Troubadour for the Lord* (New York: The Crossroad Publishing Company, 1983), p. 90.

35. Ibid., p. 92.

36. Isaiah 8:20.

37. Carolyn A. Burns, "Sheila Walsh: Radical New Waver or Rebel With a Cause?," *Contemporary Christian Magazine* (May 1984), 26.

38. John 6:67.

39. Romans 6:4.

40. "Feedback," *Contemporary Christian Magazine* (May 1984), 6.

God's Message About CCM

9

Take thou away from me the noise of thy songs.
—Amos 5:23a

A Christian's musical standards, like all his standards, must be drawn from the Bible. However, confusion exists about "Christian rock" because so many arguments *for* CCM seem to be drawn from the Bible.

After all, God has commanded us to reach the unsaved with the gospel. [1] Right? He has admonished us to praise Him with our instruments. [2] True? And He instructs us to edify and encourage each other. [3] Is that right, too? Well then, it sounds almost as if these verses suggest that—despite the problems discussed in the last chapter—CCM is probably not a bad idea. Perhaps a few performers have just gone a little too far in their enthusiasm for the Lord.

Does the Bible offer clear instruction regarding CCM? Yes! God is not the author of confusion. [4] His will is expressed in the Scriptures. Furthermore, we are told that Scripture is not only inspired (literally, "God-breathed"), but also that it "is profitable for doctrine, for reproof, for correction, for instruction in righteousness." [5] God wants us to know how to live.

Taking the Bible as our authority, let's establish some guidelines by which to evaluate Christian music. The initials "T.E.S.T." will serve as a memory jogger to help us recall four key points. Then we'll use these points to see if contemporary Christian music really represents a good alternative to rock.

Truth—Is the Message True According to Scripture?

Above all, Christian music must conform to the truth of God's Word. Isaiah 8:20b says, "If they speak not according to this word, it is because there is no light in them." In the Gospel of John, we are also told, "God is a Spirit: and they that worship him must worship him in spirit and in truth." [6] Christ even defines Himself as truth: "I am the way, the truth, and the life." [7] And in His high-priestly prayer for believers in John 17, Christ asks God to "sanctify them [Christians] through thy truth; thy word is truth."

This theme runs throughout God's instruction to us. The verses I have quoted make it clear that our presentation of Christ must be scriptural. But the same emphasis on truth is necessary as we make known God's faithfulness (exalting, Psalm 89:1), as we shun perversion of the gospel (separating, Galatians 1:7-8), and as we admonish each other with the word of Christ (teaching, Colossians 3:16).

Exalts Christ—or Man?

Psalm 89 says, "I will sing of the mercies of the Lord forever: with my mouth I will make known thy faithfulness to all generations." [8] We are also admonished, "Praise ye the Lord: for it is good to sing praises unto our God; for it is pleasant; and praise is comely." [9] The book of Acts tells us that Christ was foremost in David's mind as he composed his psalms, the Bible's songbook. "I forsaw the Lord always before my face, for he is on my right hand, that I should not be moved: Therefore did my heart rejoice, and my tongue was glad." [10]

Separate from the World?

John wrote, "Love not the world, neither the things that are in the world. If any man love the world, the love of the Father is not in him." [11] Paul wrote to the Corinthian church, "Be ye not unequally yoked together with unbelievers: for what fellowship hath righteousness with unrighteousness: and what communion hath light with darkness? . . . Come out from among them and be ye separate, saith the Lord." [12]

Romans 16:17, Galatians 1:8, and II John 7-11 tell us to avoid even those that *claim* to be the people of God but live and teach in a way that is contrary to His Word. "There be some that trouble you, and would pervert the gospel of Christ. But though we, or an angel from heaven, preach any other gospel unto you than that which we have preached unto you, let him be accursed." [13] "Many deceivers are entered into the world," II John 7 says. The Christian must try the spirits.

Teaches and Builds Up the Body of Christ?

As Christians we are told to edify one another [14] and to convey to others our knowledge of Christ so that "they shall be able to teach others also." [15] And Paul's letter to the Colossians tells us, "Let the word of Christ dwell in you richly in all wisdom; teaching and admonishing one another in psalms and hymns and spiritual songs, singing with grace in your hearts to the Lord." [16]

In short, the Christian's music should present God's truth, exalt Christ, stand separate from sin, and teach the believer—"T.E.S.T." How well does contemporary Christian music measure up to the Bible's standards? Let's look! Our survey of CCM will not be exhaustive, so don't assume groups not mentioned are acceptable. Instead, ask the Lord to use these examples to give *you* discernment.

Does the Song Present Biblical Truth?

Most fans of CCM contend that "Christian" rock presents scriptural truth, and granted, a few songs do. However, clear, biblical messages are becoming rarer in contemporary Christian recordings and performances.

As a comparison, let's first look at a hymn that makes a clear presentation of truth. The first stanza and the refrain of "I Will Praise Him" are shown below.

Hymn:	Truth Presented:
When I saw the cleansing fountain Open wide for all my sin, I obeyed the Spirit's wooing, When He said, Wilt thou be clean?	*Sinner's guilt admitted Conviction of the Spirit and call to holiness*
I will praise Him! I will praise Him! Praise the Lamb for sinners slain; Give Him glory, all ye people, For His blood can wash away each stain.	*Substitutionary atonement Glorifying Christ Christ's blood necessary for remission of sin*

God's truth (in this hymn, His truth concerning salvation) is clear. Moreover, the hymn exalts Christ, urges the listener to separate from sin, and teaches the redeemed to praise Christ for His atoning work.

Contrast this with the review quoted earlier, talking about Leon Patillo's CCM hit, "The Sky's the Limit." *Contemporary Christian Magazine* said, "The inspirational title cut [on this album] expresses the universal theme that we as individuals can do anything, when we put our minds to it, because 'the sky is the limit'." [17]

Compare that thought with the final paragraph of the *Humanist Manifesto I:*

> Man is at last becoming aware that he alone is responsible for the realization of the world of his dreams, that he has within himself the power for its achievement. [18]

Patillo's song presents no biblical message. In too much of his music we find potential confusion—rather than communication—of God's truth. Patillo isn't deliberately preaching the humanist's position. He doesn't have to; the lack of a clear gospel testimony in the song lets the listener fill in almost any message he or she wants to hear.

The message of some of Amy Grant's songs is equally unclear. One example, "I Love a Lonely Day" on Grant's best-selling *Age to Age* album, is simply a love song written by Grant's husband, Gary Chapman. On National Public Radio's "All Things Considered," an interviewer asked Amy about the secular, even sexy, quality of many of her songs. Amy replied that the listener could apply the message of such songs "to any relationship he or she chooses." [19] Remember, however, that CCM claims to be more than just sanitized rock. If the lyrics are so vague that they apply to almost any relationship, will the listener hear God's truth? Or will God's message of love for the lost be missed—as Paul asked the Corinthians, "If the trumpet give an uncertain sound, who shall prepare himself . . . ?" [20]

Confusion and ambiguity—is this the message of contemporary Christian music? Not entirely. Some songs actually present a message *contrary* to God's Word. Steve Taylor's theology in a song on the album *Meltdown* is just as bad. "Jenny" tells of a girl who fell into sin and committed suicide instead of seeking forgiveness through the blood of Christ. The cleansing and forgiveness for which David prayed in Psalm 51 is never mentioned. How can Steve Taylor's story convey the message of Christ's love and hope to sinners? The answer is that it doesn't!

The Scripture on Donna Summer's album, *She Works Hard for the Money,* hints that the listener should expect a Christian worldview. Yet "Unconditional Love," a song with nominally Christian lyrics, tells us that we are not to try to change our fellowman. True, God, and not man, is the One who changes lives, but this song focuses on a fuzzy, non-discerning "love" that could keep Christians from exhorting men and women to come out of their sin. Another song, a duet with Matthew Ward of 2nd Chapter of Acts, shows love between a man and woman as causing them to abandon all control.

Even Keith Green, now deceased, whose life showed many signs of true faith in Christ, had his theological problems. Once again, CCM's emphasis on the *music* seems to have resulted in too little *attention to the message.* In Keith's popular recording, "Your Love Broke Through," salvation is presented as being both easy and something the Christian will never doubt. No repentance is presented. Green only tells of his life being wasted and unsatisfying until God's love broke through. While that is part of any Christian's testimony, Green's song does not go on to make a clear presentation of the gospel. How is the sinner to know when "God's love breaks through"? Is it just a feeling? What is expected of the sinner? What is involved in asking Christ in?

These questions are not answered by the song, and while we cannot expect the song to present a systematic study of all Bible doctrines, we should expect an adequate presentation of how men and women are saved.

Foggy presentation of the gospel leads to "easy-believism," quick decisions, false conversions, and eternal doom. This vagueness and the attitude behind Amy Grant's statement noted in the last chapter ("I'm not out to convert anybody") seem to contradict CCM's professed aim of getting out the gospel and falls far short of the Bible's admonition in Mark 16:15, "Go ye into all the world, and preach the gospel to every creature."

Too many young people may already be substituting a feeling—an emotional, musical experience—for a real knowledge of Christ. A pro-CCM participant in a recent radio talk show even offered that defense when pressed to justify "Christian" rock. "What about what I *feel*?" he said. "I've been blessed!" [21]

But some will say, "Christian music doesn't always need to be serious. Sometimes it's just good, clean entertainment." However, entertainment is for the purpose of diversion or distraction. Its purpose is to draw the mind *away* from the cares of the moment. Is that the proper occupation of Christian music, or should it draw us *toward* God? And even in drawing the mind toward God, our focus must be the truth of God's Word—presented with sufficient completeness and clarity.

Does the Song Exalt Christ?

When we apply our T.E.S.T. to contemporary Christian music, we also find a strong emphasis on man—not Christ. "Raining on the Inside" by Amy Grant is a good example, though certainly not the only one. In this song, she focuses on the loneliness that she experiences.

The goal is *her* peace of mind and release from pain.

This sort of introspective, man-centered approach is typical of CCM. Debby Boone's "You Light Up My Life" was an early signal that the individual believer would become the focus of CCM rather than the Saviour. Songs like "Wait Upon the Lord" by the Imperials, "Mansion Builder" by 2nd Chapter of Acts, "Mainstream" by Michael and Stormie Omartian, and "Carry On" by White Heart all emphasize the believer's needs, the believer's feelings, and the benefits sought by the believer. These are not simple testimony songs, like "Since I Have Been Redeemed." Christian testimony reveals the complete work of Christ, and the focus is Christ. These (and other similar songs) focus on man and leave the impression of an incomplete work by Christ.

Contrast these songs with "Holy, Holy, Holy," "O Worship the King," or "Praise to the Lord, the Almighty." Even while acknowledging God's benefits to the believer, "Praise to the Lord" maintains a consistent Godward look.

Praise to the Lord, the Almighty, the King of creation!
O my soul, praise Him, for He is thy health and salvation!
Come ye who hear, Now to His great throne draw near;
Join me in glad adoration.

Praise to the Lord, who o'er all things so wondrously reigneth,
Shelters thee under His wings, yea, so gently sustaineth!
Hast thou not seen all that is needful hath been
Granted in what He ordaineth.

Praise to the Lord, who doth prosper thy work and defend
  thee;
Surely His goodness and mercy here daily attend thee.
Ponder anew what the Almighty can do,
He who with love doth befriend thee.

Praise to the Lord, O let all that is in me adore Him!
All that hath life and breath, come now with praises before
  Him.

Let the Amen sound from His people again,
Gladly for aye we adore Him.

When CCM does focus on God, the music is often totally unsuitable for the message of exaltation. Good Christian music should strive for the most effective possible union of music and message. Instead, too much contemporary Christian music has words and music that clash—like a dignified gentleman in a tuxedo (the words) playing with the toys in a nursery. As one writer put it, "When inappropriate music is coupled with a fine text, the effect is to make the text ludicrous." [22]

In *Modern Art and the Death of a Culture*, H. R. Rookmaaker points out that

> a work of art has to be in keeping with the place or occasion for which it is made, or the function it has to fulfill. You are not going to paint Christ on the cross in the style of a cartoon. Indeed, some "Christian" art is at fault here: certain religious magazines sometimes portray Christ and biblical scenes in a way that is below standard, with a style that is too cheap. What is acceptable in a brochure for a new vacuum cleaner is wrong for such subjects, unless we are going to reduce Christianity to the level of commerciality and profit. [23]

Christian music must meet the test of "appropriateness" if it is to exalt Christ properly. The Saviour cannot be neatly tucked into a contemporary capsule, complete with slang phrases and a rock beat. He is the Son of the eternal, most high God, before whom men have trembled when just a glimpse of His holiness was seen. Too often, CCM'ers appear to have lost all sense of majesty, of solemnity, and of the reverence due God.

Is the Style Separate from the World?

Several years ago, country singer Willie Nelson recorded an album of hymns. The highest compliment the record reviewers seemed able to pay Nelson was to note, "Nelson has given the old church songs the *regular* Willie Nelson treatment, performing them in the same existential way(s) he performs songs officially designated as 'commercial' or 'secular.' His band, one of the jauntiest and best bar bands in Texas, plays here the way it plays in honky tonks. . . ." [24]

Strangely enough, the attitude of many Christians today is not much different from the attitude of that reviewer. Could rock ever be used to exalt Christ? The answer is no. Art and music always reflect a particular view on life and the world. "Deeply felt values [are expressed] . . . through *the way* the theme and the subject matter [are] handled. Thus, even junk art and punk rock say something very definite, very deliberately." [25] What rock is saying in today's culture disqualifies it as a vehicle for spiritual communication.

After salvation, God expects the Christian to "walk in newness of life." [26] Paul tells us in II Corinthians 5:17 that the Christian is to be a "new creature: old things are passed away." To drag cultural baggage from the old life into our Christian lives suggests to lost people that there has been no real change.

Despite this, CCM fans often argue that music is nothing more than vibrations—audible frequencies and metric patterns combined to create melody, harmony, and rhythm. By definition, since these "building blocks" are neutral, all music itself is therefore also supposed to be neutral or amoral.

Reduced to its smallest component parts, music *is* amoral. There is nothing inherently wrong with a 440 Hz vibration or a dotted quarter note followed by an eighth note. The same could be said for any letter of the alphabet, a drop of paint, or a particle of clay. But as soon as a human being combines any of these "building blocks," the creative process has begun and the resulting creation always reflects a particular view of life.

For this reason, the Christian cannot sanitize rock. Even if we ignored the worldly associations of rock (and we cannot), its musical origin springs from a view of life altogether different from the Christian's. Because Christ must be the focal point of our music, the style must never overshadow Him or draw attention to itself.

There is one final issue related to separation. How far can Christian performers go out into the world to perform? For example, would it be all right for a CCM performer to accept a contract to perform in a night-club? After all, separation but not isolation—isn't that the cry of many contemporary Christian music performers?

Psalm 137:4 says, "How shall we sing the Lord's song in a strange land?" When the Psalmist asks, "How shall we sing . . . ," he is clearly expressing the sadness felt by the people and asking, "How can we sing at all?" But more than that, his question recognizes the inappropriateness and lack of separation that would be demonstrated by singing the Lord's songs "in a strange land." Their captors would understand little (if anything) of God's salvation, His daily guidance and mercies, and His love. In the same way, the Christian should find it inappropriate to sing the Lord's song in a strange land—that is, in any place that would compromise his or her testimony.

Does the Song Teach or Build Up the Believer?

In addition to presenting the truth of God's Word, exalting Christ, and standing separate from the world, good Christian music should teach or build up the believer. Yet imagine the following monologue:

Matthew: Hearing the Lord's voice was a real job for me, you know? It was like . . .

Funny voice:	"Matthew, I know you're in there. Come out!"
Matthew:	... you know, and uh ... [Audience laughter] ... my walk started ... began to be really, really apathetic, it was just kind of, you know, ...
Singsong voice:	"Well, I'm a Christian, hallelujah; go to church, whatever."
Matthew:	... Things like that ... [Laughter], but uh, ... [More laughter] ... you know ... And uh, finally the Lord decided that He had had enough of that from me and He goes,
Speaking for the Lord:	"OK, c'mon. I want more outta you than that."
Matthew:	Ever since that time, you know, my walk with the Lord's been really gettin' a lot better—I mean, I just praise God. . .He's been doin' so many things in my life, it's [Choked shout] WOW! [More laughter] You know ... I'm just gettin' really excited. Anyway, I'd just like to share this song. . . .[27]

Edifying? Not really, but this is an actual testimony presented by a popular CCM performer—Matthew Ward of 2nd Chapter of Acts. Probably only comic Mike Warnke could rival this monologue, and Warnke's "humor" approaches blasphemy.

Nevertheless, contemporary Christian music performers place great importance on "sharing," a CCM buzzword usually preferred to "giving testimony" or "witnessing." Personal sharing gets a lot of attention, both on record and in concert. In fact, even record reviewers have begun to object. "About 9 of the 44 minutes on the album are taken up with ... [the] altar call, mercifully shorter than his usual concert message.

... While I firmly believe in the 'foolishness of preaching,' I feel cheated when forced to listen to it on an album that I bought for the music." [28] The writer's annoyance is understandable. Trying to make up for the lack of a clear message in a song by adding something like Ward's monologue or some sort of insipid "sharing" only irritates the listener who is looking for substance.

Very little contemporary Christian music exhorts or reproves. Few songs encourage any sort of heart-searching or application of their message. How do some of the introspective, feelings-oriented songs you may know compare with "Am I a Soldier of the Cross?"

Am I a soldier of the cross, A follower of the Lamb,
And shall I fear to own His cause, or blush to speak His name?

Must I be carried to the skies on flowery beds of ease,
While others fought to win the prize, and sailed through
 bloody seas?

Are there no foes for me to face? Must I not stem the flood?
Is this vile world a friend to grace, to help me on to God?

Sure I must fight, if I would reign; Increase my courage, Lord;
I'll bear the toil, endure the pain, supported by Thy Word.

In "Am I a Soldier of the Cross?" there are lessons to be learned. But what do we learn from a monologue that ends "WOW! You know . . . I'm just gettin' really excited"? What do we learn from Amy Grant's introspective "Raining on the Inside" (and other songs like it)? Good Christian music has substance because the word of Christ dwells in the believer "richly in all wisdom." [29] Our music must show others the eternal wisdom that Christ has shown us.

"Yield Yourselves unto God" [30]

It is impossible to yield an old, unregenerate nature to Christ. You can resolve to give up rock or CCM, but unless you know Christ your old nature won't stay "yielded."

However, enslavement to sin ended at the cross for the Christian. The old nature is still there, but we are energized by a new Source of life. And just as we don't "reconnect" our lives to that dark source of whom we were once servants, the Christian ought not reconnect with the trappings of the old life.

Sadly, that's just what some professing Christians recommend. In his book *Rock Reconsidered*, Steve Lawhead even takes Paul's words to the Romans and attempts to explain that they don't mean what they say. Lawhead says, "When the apostle Paul warns 'do not be conformed to this world' (Romans 12:2), he is talking more about character than conduct. Limiting our participation in society is not his aim." [31]

Paul said nothing of the sort. Character, as the sum total of our beliefs and attitudes, *governs our conduct!* To divide the two is absurd. Thought always precedes conduct, and our beliefs determine the direction of our thoughts. To try to pull character and conduct apart is to suggest we can think one way but act another.

The desire to live a holy life ought to follow your salvation. Indeed, such a desire is a mark of regeneration. And to live a holy life, you almost certainly will have to limit your participation in a corrupt and sinful society. "But now being made free from sin, and become servants to God, ye have your fruit unto holiness, and the end everlasting life." [32]

Summing Up

In the first section of this book (chapters one through six), we saw the need for a *personal* separation from evil. The rock subculture is so thoroughly corrupt that the believer must choose to either associate with sin or to follow the Bible's instruction to avoid the "appearance of evil." [33]

In the second section (chapters seven through nine), the need for personal *and ecclesiastical* separation became apparent. We must sometimes separate from those who call themselves Christians but do not live and speak according to God's Word. "Mark them which cause divisions and offences contrary to the doctrine which ye have learned; and avoid them." [34]

Paul, under the inspiration of the Holy Spirit, wrote even stronger words to Timothy and Titus. Speaking of people much like those we see in the CCM movement, he said, "The time will come when they will not endure sound doctrine." [35] What were believers to do? "A man that is an heretick after the first and second admonition reject; knowing that he that is such is subverted, and sinneth, being condemned of himself." [36]

These are hard words. We don't like to think that we may have to separate from others who call themselves Christians. Yet, we have clear teaching in the Bible that tells us this ecclesiastical separation will be necessary. We cannot be "one" with those who do not believe the Bible. We cannot support those who do not live according to the Bible. We cannot agree with those who do not agree with God.

If you have taken the first step and have given up rock, I encourage you now to take the second step and separate from CCM's compromise of God's truth and Bible standards. Chapter ten offers some practical suggestions as to where to start.

Endnotes

1. Matthew 28:19-20.

2. Psalm 150:3–5.

3. I Thessalonians 5:11, Romans 14:19.

4. I Corinthians 14:33.

5. II Timothy 3:16.

6. John 4:24.

7. John 14:6a.

8. Psalm 89:1.

9. Psalm 147:1.

10. Acts 2:25-26a. Read through all of Acts 2:25-31.

11. I John 2:15.

12. Read II Corinthians 6:14-18.

13. Galatians 1:7b-8.

14. I Thessalonians 5:11.

15. II Timothy 2:2.

16. Colossians 3:16.

17. Tim A. Smith, "Music/Records," *Contemporary Christian Magazine* (May 1984), 39.

18. *The Humanist Manifesto I* (Buffalo, New York: Prometheus Books, 1973), p. 10.

19. "All Things Considered," *National Public Radio* (aired in Atlanta, Georgia, on May 23, 1984).

20. I Corinthians 14:8.

21. "Insight," Radio Station WMUU (aired in Greenville, South Carolina, on June 7, 1984).

22. Danny M. Sweatt, *Church Music: Sense and Nonsense* (Greenville, SC: Bob Jones University Press, 1981), p. 14.

23. H. R. Rookmaaker, *Modern Art and the Death of a Culture* (London: InterVarsity Press, 1973), p. 238. Rookmaaker expresses this point well, but his work cannot be given a blanket endorsement. He makes statements that are unacceptable to the fundamental Christian because he fails to grasp the biblical doctrine of separation.

24. Noel Coppage, "Preacher Willie Nelson," *Stereo Review* (February 1977), 88.

25. H. R. Rookmaaker, *Modern Art and the Death of a Culture* (London: InterVarsity Press, 1973), p. 18.

26. Romans 6:4.

27. Matthew Ward, from the album *Together Live,* by 2nd Chapter of Acts and Michael and Stormie Omartian (1983, Sparrow Records).

28. Devlin Donaldson, "Music/Records," *Contemporary Christian Magazine* (April 1984), 40.

29. Colossians 3:16.

30. Romans 6:13.

31. Steve Lawhead, *Rock Reconsidered* (Downers Grove, Illinois: InterVarsity Press, 1981), p. 94.

32. Romans 6:22.

33. I Thessalonians 5:22.

34. Romans 16:17.

35. II Timothy 4:3a.

36. Titus 3:10–11.

Section Three:
The Christian's
Response

Life After Rock
10

Surely, surely, slumber is more sweet than toil.
—Alfred, Lord Tennyson

In the last nine chapters, you've seen the folly of contemporary music. You're ready to try it God's way, and you're open to His leading. What next?

First, be thankful for the Lord's patient guidance. We claimed His promise from Psalm 32:8 as we began. "I will instruct thee and teach thee in the way which thou shalt go: I will guide thee with mine eye." If God has given you the grace to make a break with rock, you have much for which to thank Him. No longer slumbering, you can echo the words from Robert Murray McCheyne's hymn, "When This Passing World."

> Chosen not for good in me;
> Wakened up from wrath to flee;
> Hidden in the Saviour's side;
> By the Spirit sanctified.

But for weeks, or perhaps even months, you may feel Tennyson had more insight in this case than McCheyne. Sometimes it feels much easier to "slumber" than to be awakened to a bad situation. Although God enables some to make a clean break with rock and never look back, for many whose eyes are opened to the problem, giving up contemporary music is still a difficult battle.

Can the battle be won? Yes! However, you must first resolve—and promise the Lord—that you *are* finished with rock. Why? Because many of us who have given up rock miss the music tremendously for a while. Some even compare the difficulty to quitting smoking for the smoker or giving up drinking for the alcoholic. A few people get immediate victory, but for others the decision to quit must be renewed daily.

But what else can be done? Surely there must be some alternatives, something to fill the void left by giving up the music that has been an important part of your life for years. There are no simple answers, no ready replacements, but several suggestions can be made. [1]

Get Closer to God

This seems so obvious, and yet many Christians make difficult decisions and then try to carry them out in their own strength. First, resolve to give up rock by trusting God to enable you. "I can do all things through Christ which strengtheneth me." [2] Go to God in prayer and ask Him to give you that strength *daily.* Decide to give up contemporary music, but renew that decision every day, one day at a time.

Second, fill your mind with Scripture. Most Christians know that they ought to memorize God's Word. However, the ability to call verses to mind will be even more important than usual during the days and weeks following your decision to give up rock. Such verses will provide reassurance that God is eager to help, and you will also find your appreciation for the traditional hymns growing in almost direct proportion to the amount of Scripture memory you do. That's not surprising, since the best hymns are based on biblical texts. If you are persistent about memorizing Scripture, you will be amazed how many hymns will open up to reveal new depths of meaning, based on your study of God's Word.

Learn to Play an Instrument

Some may think this is an unusual suggestion, but it can be one of the most effective ways possible to change your musical perspective. For those who have only been listeners, learning an instrument creates a new appreciation for the skills necessary to play well. Suddenly recording artists who were never of interest before become an important part of your record collection—because they demonstrate the skills, the various techniques, you are seeking to master.

Obviously this suggestion presupposes that you will build a record collection from the standard repertoire—not from contemporary music. However, learning the standard repertoire is effective even for those who already *know* how to play an instrument and may have performed in a rock band or a CCM group. Guitarists, for example, can find much to challenge their skills in listening to Segovia, Bream, or Christopher Parkening. Keyboard players have a vast selection of music from which to choose. Even hard-core rock drummers can find satisfaction in channeling their abilities toward symphonic percussion and its musical literature.

Give Other Styles of Music the Time You Gave Rock

Your preference for contemporary music, and for certain groups, did not develop overnight. In fact, if you were involved with rock for very long, it's likely your preferences developed over a period of years—and even changed from time to time.

You cannot expect to become knowledgeable about

a new musical field any more quickly than you did about rock. Since the standard repertoire extends back for hundreds of years, finding the music you like most will take a while. Spend time exploring! Ask for advice. Join a record club. (The addresses of two good ones are included in the Appendix entitled "Listening Suggestions.") Visit your public library. Libraries often have records that can be borrowed. Take advantage of this service. Attend concerts. Sit up front, close to the orchestra or performers. Even the most confirmed rock fan will be impressed by the immediacy and presence of a first-rate symphony orchestra performing in a hall with good acoustics.

Squelch any preconceived notions you may have about what kinds of music you like and dislike, but be careful about replacing rock with something worse! The Bible tells about an evil spirit that goes out of a man and wanders about seeking rest. Finding no rest, the spirit returns to the man, only to realize his former dwelling place is empty and has been swept clean. The result is that the spirit "taketh with himself seven other spirits more wicked than himself, and they enter in and dwell there: and the last state of that man is worse than the first." [3]

When you sweep your life clean, approach new musical styles with caution. For example, except in the sense that it still falls under the heading of "contemporary music," we have not talked about country music. To sweep out rock and usher in country, as some have done, would serve no good purpose. You must always use caution and ask the Lord for discernment, in this area as in *all* areas of your life.

Sing the Psalms

Although the Psalms have been largely forgotten by today's church musicians, in previous centuries and in

Europe even today the Psalter is the Christian's songbook. Ask your choir director or minister of music where you might secure a book containing the Psalms set to metre. If you can't locate one where you live, write the publisher listed in the Appendix entitled "Additional Reading" at the end of this book.

Even those hymns that paraphrase a biblical text are partly of man's contriving. The Psalms, inspired by the Holy Spirit, when properly translated and set to music, are perhaps the closest to heavenly songs Christians will know until we are with the Lord.

Be Careful About Your Radio and Television Listening Habits

Radio and TV always demand vigilance on the part of the Christian. However, contemporary music's influence on our culture and on the broadcast media is so pervasive that you may find yourself ensnared by rock again unless you are watchful. Advertisements, theme songs, and even the background music for some news and sports features may be a problem while you are working to develop new listening habits.

If this sounds extreme, consider the alternatives. Is it worth taking a chance—only to fall back into the sin and satanism of rock music that grieves and angers God? And be cautious while shopping as well. Record stores are an obvious problem, since many maintain a playlist that assures exposure for the current hits. But many other stores in most shopping malls program popular music for their customers, particularly in young people's clothing stores (or clothing departments within larger department stores). If the contemporary sound still attracts you, find other merchants with whom you can shop, or consider politely asking store and department managers if they would be willing to change their musical programming. It wouldn't hurt to write or call your local radio or TV station if they play rock music and let them know that you do not appreciate their music.

Pray

Finally, pray that the Lord will raise up godly Christian artists to provide acceptable music. The Bible makes it clear that music was an important part of worship in centuries past. God can renew Christian music. We cannot be satisfied with imitating the world. Christ's people—more than all others—should have the spiritual and creative resources necessary to write fresh, imaginative expressions of worship and praise.

Are we going to admit that the world has a monopoly on new sounds or imaginative expression? No! To do that would say that we really don't know the Divine Source of all that is creative, all that is good. Pray that the Lord will use men and women to create a new song, a song worthy of His name.

Endnotes

1. For much of the material in the following section, I am indebted to Judy Gamble's article, "Home-Made Music," which served as a valuable catalyst during a time when I was seeking alternatives for young people who were giving up rock. This article appeared in *FAITH for the Family* magazine, May/June 1984, published by Bob Jones University, Greenville, SC 29614.

2. Philippians 4:13.

3. Matthew 12:43-45.

Epilogue: Goliath's Challenge Revisited

... Is there not a cause?
—I Samuel 17:29

The armies had been in the field for weeks. On a mountain to one side of the valley of Elah, the Philistines encamped. On the other side gathered the armies of Israel.

Each day for almost six weeks Goliath, champion of the Philistines, left camp to stand before the Israelites and shout, "I defy the armies of Israel this day" (I Samuel 17:10). Each day, Goliath's challenge went unanswered.

David's brothers had witnessed this sight. However, it was not until David asked, "Who is this uncircumcised Philistine, that he should defy the armies of the living God?"[1] that his brothers were convicted of their cowardice and silence. For Goliath's challenge was uttered not just against the armies of Israel, but against their God as well.

"I will smite thee," David answered Goliath, ". . . that all the earth may know that there is a God in Israel."[2] But who will answer Goliath's challenge today? The heathen still rage,[3] though now they're found at rock concerts, on record, and over radio and TV. But where are the Christian soldiers? Are we no longer able to "war a good warfare?" [4] Perhaps not, for many have gone over to the camp of the enemy. Our churches are full of contemporary "Christian" sounds, and our homes, the music of the devil.

Is There Not a Cause?

> Blow ye the trumpet in Zion, and sound an alarm in my holy mountain: let all the inhabitants of the land tremble: for the day of the Lord cometh, for it is nigh at hand (Joel 2:1).

David, as a youth, was a very unlikely candidate for the champion of Israel on the day he slew Goliath, but all others had feared to answer the challenge. You only need to open your ears to hear the continuing ring of Goliath's challenge today.

What can you do? First, if you have one foot in each camp, "come out from among them, and be ye separate, saith the Lord." [5] "I would not that ye should have fellowship with devils." [6] Maybe this is the first time you have been urged to be a separated, holy Christian. Heed the Bible's instruction.

Second, sound an alarm. Tell others what you have learned. Despite ample evidence, most Christians have little idea how strongly Satan has established himself in the lives and music of many contemporary performers; the unsaved have no notion whatsoever.

David answered Goliath's challenge, and "when the Philistines saw their champion was dead, they fled," [7] and the men of Israel drove their armies back! We ought to pray that such a victory might be won today against the forces of evil. May this book be used by God to encourage you to stand, as a good soldier of Christ, in the face of Goliath's challenge.

Endnotes

1. I Samuel 17:26.

2. I Samuel 17:46.

3. Psalm 2:1.

4. I Timothy 1:18.

5. II Corinthians 6:17.

6. I Corinthians 10:20.

7. I Samuel 17:51.

Appendixes

Appendix One

Quick-Reference Questions and Answers

In telling people about Christ, the Christian soon finds that a small number of predictable objections to the gospel are raised. These objections usually come from a lost person under conviction who hopes he or she can throw the conversation off track. If the person succeeds, attention is no longer focused upon his response to the gospel.

For example, one hears questions like, "What is God going to do about the heathen who have never heard the gospel?" and "How can God be a loving God if He permits war and sickness?" By equipping himself to answer a dozen or so common questions and objections, the Christian can keep such conversations focused on Christ and the sinner's need for Christ as Saviour.

Similarly, in talking to rock fans about contemporary music, a limited number of predictable objections are raised. These are listed in chapter six. To enable you to find the information you need more quickly, this reference guide has been developed. Listed below are the objections, followed by a brief answer, along with the page number in chapter six (if you want more information).

126

Christians see listening to rock as being "guilty by association." [Page 53]

That's right. The Bible not only forbids participation in sin, but association with it, too. See I Thessalonians 5:22 and Romans 14:16,18.

It's all an image. [Pages 54-55]

Concerts, MTV, and rock stars' lives indicate the sin associated with rock is more than an image. See Matthew 12:34-35.

Our perspective changes. [Pages 55-56]

God's standards are absolute and unchanging. See II Timothy 3:16 and Jeremiah 6:16. (A variation of this argument is, "What about the sinful 'classical composers'?")

I don't listen to the lyrics. [Pages 56-57]

Whether you listen to them or not, you are associated with sin. There is also danger of subconsciously taking in information. See I Corinthians 3:16-17a.

The loudness/beat has no effect on me. [Pages 57-58]

Concert level sound can damage your hearing. However, beyond that, even fans of rock admit that "something happens" when the music starts. Christians must not permit their minds and bodies to be controlled by anything other than the Holy Spirit.

It's just a matter of taste. [Pages 58-59]

That might be true if we were talking about musical structure or form. But the issue is holiness, and that is not subject to "taste." See Ezekiel 44:23.

To suppress rock is censorship. [Pages 59-60]

"Censorship," or choosing what we permit to come into our lives, is a thoroughly biblical idea. See I Thessalonians 5:21 and Philippians 4:8.

I'm strong enough. [Pages 60-61]

No human being is strong enough to withstand the attacks of the devil, except in Christ's strength. The

Bible warns about this presumptuous attitude—thinking we can stand. See I Corinthians 10:12. (Christian "liberty" is another cloak for this argument. See Romans 14:1-15:1 and I Corinthians 8:1-13.)

Rock is an important barometer of our culture. [Pages 61-62]

Christians are not to follow every cultural trend. See Ephesians 4:14 and Romans 16:19.

There are some good messages/songs/etc. [Pages 62-63]

Even if there are, we cannot find and enjoy them without being contaminated by the bad messages/songs/etc. It is the pizza or poison problem again. We must remain separate from sin.

What about "soft rock"? [Pages 63-65]

This is a variation of "There are some good messages." In addition to the pizza or poison problem, (1) the message of soft music may not be "soft," (2) soft performers don't often stay soft, and (3) the listener develops an appetite for more of the contemporary sound.

But Christians are to be the "salt." [Page 65]

Salt should prevent and arrest decay, but Christians are not acting like salt if they participate in corrupt contemporary trends (like rock) in order to reach those involved. See John 17:15. Christ stressed separation from sin.

Appendix Two

The Back-Masking Controversy

"Back-masking" or "backward masking" refers to a recording technique that many claim is used to conceal messages in rock songs. The message is said to be hidden by recording it forward (normally) but then playing it backward while mixing the final version of the song that is to contain the hidden message. This backward message is "masked" by the normal voices and instruments, as well as the fact that—if the message is heard at all—it can only be heard backwards when the record is played in the normal way.

The purpose of this brief discussion is to acknowledge the issue and present both sides of the argument. Because back-masking has received a great deal of attention, you should know what the term means and have the background necessary to discuss it with others.

Christians differ on this issue. Some say the technique is never used or that, if it is used, we are not affected by backward messages. Other Christians say that they have heard the messages "decoded" (by taping records said to contain these messages and then playing the tape backwards). Christians who say that this technique is used are concerned about listeners who are being manipulated by these messages without realizing it.

This technique was mentioned briefly when we discussed the group Black Oak Arkansas in chapter four. Others who are supposed to have used it include the Beatles (on their *Abbey Road* album), the Electric Light Orchestra (particularly on *Eldorado*), Styx, and Pink Floyd. The basis for the technique is found in studies of subliminal perception. "Subliminal" refers to something done so that its effects are below the level of consciousness. "Perception," of course, is simply our ability to perceive—to receive information.

Early experiments in subliminal perception used a tachistoscope. This device, which works something like a high-speed slide projector, flashed a message on the screen in motion picture theaters. Viewers were not aware of the messages, which were designed to convince them that they were hungry and should buy popcorn or a soft drink. However, apparently the messages worked! During one six-week test, popcorn sales increased by almost sixty percent and drink sales by about twenty percent. Backward masking is said to accomplish the same results—planting information in our minds without our awareness. However, the absence of documented studies that demonstrate our minds can "decode" backward messages causes some to question whether this technique works in the same way as the tachistoscope.

Record producers and industry executives deny that backward masking exists. Electronic manipulation of sound is commonplace (including effects created by recording normally but then mixing in the same material played in reverse). But no one in the industry acknowledges deliberately using such techniques to plant subliminal messages. If messages are mixed into songs, some say that it is only because groups accused of back-masking have sold *more* records as a result of listeners seeking to find such messages.

So, we are back to the basic question: do rock groups really use backward masking to hide immoral or satanic messages? Certainly Satan uses rock as a means to accomplish his purposes. If backward masking or any other technique promotes his goals, it would be foolish to think that Satan would ignore it. The technology exists, and he certainly desires to influence listeners. As a result, the thinking Christian must acknowledge the possibility.

However, even if back-masking were clearly proven to have an effect upon our behavior, it would only provide one more reason to shun rock. More than enough problems exist when listening to rock *played forward*! These clearly evident problems should be enough to make the Christian stand apart from evil and seek a closer relationship with Christ.

Appendix Three

Additional Reading

Some readers will want more information about contemporary music, and a number of sources exist. Some of these sources are useful. Others are not so useful and may actually be dangerous—unless the reader's own convictions about rock are already firmly established. A few simply should not be consulted because of the prevalence of objectionable material (nudity, vulgar language, and more).

This bibliography should help guide you in selecting references. Pay close attention to the comments about each item. Read these comments in the same way you would read a book review. You should understand that they are only one writer's opinion. Nevertheless, you may avoid a bad experience (or a waste of time) by knowing something about these sources before using them.

Books

The most important book you can read is the Bible. The key to giving up rock is not really a matter of learning more about it. People smoke cigarettes, drink alcohol, and take drugs, even though they know about the dangers associated with these practices. The key to giving up rock is to see Christ—His holiness, His love, and His sacrifice of Himself to redeem men and women. When we really see Him, we will seek to please Him. Once such a heart attitude exists, there is no need for more information about the evils of rock.

As I mentioned in chapter ten, singing the Psalms is especially helpful for the person trying to escape from an addiction to rock music. Our minds have a special capacity to retain words arranged in metrical form and accompanied by music. We all seem to remember the jingles we hear in TV and radio commercials, and something of the same principle applies here. Having memorized psalms in this way, you will be able to meditate on them and soak up the purifying truth of God. If you cannot find a psalter in your local bookstore, write to the following address for the title *Psalter in Metre* (revised edition, staff version):

> Oxford University Press
> 16-00 Pollitt Drive
> Fair Lawn, NJ 07410

However, pastors, teachers, parents, and young people who are seeking to counsel others about music may want additional information. Because contemporary music changes quickly, these references are only as current as their publication dates. Take that into account when using them.

Bill, J. Brent. *Rock and Roll: Proceed with Caution.* Old Tappan, New Jersey: Fleming H. Revell Company, 1984. Bill has tried to take a balanced, "reasoned" approach to rock. He makes a number of good points against it. However, despite the title, he finishes with a soft position on the issue and a favorable stance toward CCM. The book even contains a chart called "Sounds Like . . ." that is designed to help listeners find a CCM group that sounds just like their favorite rock group.

Boa, Kenneth, and Livgren, Kerry. *Seeds of Change.* Westchester, Illinois: Crossway Books, 1983. Livgren is known for his work with the rock group Kansas. The book is supposed to present his spiritual quest, but it leaves the impression of a self-serving effort. Livgren offers several of the usual defenses for staying involved with rock. There is little original here, but it may be interesting to the reader as background information.

Goldman, Albert. *Elvis.* New York: McGraw-Hill Company, 1981. A too-thorough biography containing descriptions of Elvis's worst periods of degeneracy.

Harrell, Robert D. *Martin Luther: His Music, His Message.* Greenville, South Carolina: Musical Ministries, 1980. A short book that answers one common objection voiced by those who favor CCM—the misconception that much of the church music of past centuries was based upon popular drinking songs and worldly music. You should acquire a copy of this reference.

Herman, Gary. *Rock 'n' Roll Babylon.* New York: G. P. Putnam's Sons, 1982. A picture-and-text treatment of the worst aspects of rock. Nudity and vulgar language will make this book among the most offensive to the Christian, so there should be little or no reason for seeking out this reference.

Larson, Bob. *Rock: For Those Who Listen to the Words and Don't Like What They Hear.* Wheaton, Illinois: Tyndale House Publishers, 1983. In this book, Larson takes the strongest position against rock offered in any of these references. However, he is weak on the CCM issue and may confuse some readers as a result.

Lawhead, Steve. *Rock Reconsidered.* Downers Grove, Illinois: InterVarsity Press, 1981. This is a not-so-subtle defense of rock. The author suggests that Christians should reconsider any "narrow" views they may hold that condemn all rock music. The book attempts to answer all the usual arguments against rock. The book should not be read by someone who is having difficulty seeing the biblical issues involved with rock. Because the author's arguments are not sound and he contradicts himself at several points, this book would only confuse a reader whose convictions about contemporary music are not settled.

O'Neill, Dan. *Troubadour for the Lord.* New York: The Crossroad Publishing Company, 1983. This book on John

Michael Talbot is one of numerous biographies of CCM performers. You can find others at a Christian bookstore. O'Neill treats Talbot in a favorable light but covers his divorce and his conversion to Roman Catholicism.

Pareles, John, and Romanowski, Patricia. *The Rolling Stone Encyclopedia of Rock and Roll.* New York: Rolling Stone Press/Summit Books, 1983. This 600-plus-page volume is one of the most useful guides available, detailing who's who in the world of rock. It lists virtually every important performer and group between 1950 and its publication date in 1983. Obviously, it takes a positive view of rock, and there is also some offensive language in the book. Nevertheless, for parents, pastors, and teachers who need to know the group names, biographical information, and major records, it is a valuable source of information.

Sweatt, Danny M. *Church Music: Sense and Nonsense.* Greenville, South Carolina: Bob Jones University Press, 1981. This brief book (33 pages of text) warns about the current trends in church music. It will be a useful companion to other references you own dealing with Christian music.

Magazines

Billboard, 1515 Broadway, New York, NY 10036. *Billboard* calls itself "The International Newsweekly of Music and Home Entertainment." It contains the most influential charts of musical hits (including the Hot 100, which is a registered trademark). The magazine also features record reviews and advertisements, along with editorial material about trends in the music industry. *Billboard* can be difficult to find, although some newsstands carry it. The magazine may contain material offensive to Christian readers.

Contemporary Christian Magazine, P. O. Box 6300, Laguna Hills, CA 92654. This magazine is the best source of information about CCM performers. Despite the magazine's support for CCM, the articles, record reviews, and advertisements provide first-hand evidence that should cause the Christian to see the lack of any scriptural basis for CCM's philosophy.

FAITH for the Family, Greenville, SC 29614. Published for

Bible-believing Christians, this magazine often contains helpful articles dealing with the ecumenical and charismatic movements, which are so much a part of CCM. You may also want to write for a back issue, May/June 1984, containing Judy Gamble's article, "Home-Made Music." It suggests a number of ways to build good listening habits.

Rolling Stone, Straight Arrow Publishing, 745 Fifth Avenue, New York, NY 10151. *Rolling Stone* began as a magazine devoted almost exclusively to rock music and rock music personalities. It later broadened its editorial content but is now returning to a more music-oriented format. It is a good source for interviews with contemporary performers. Many libraries will have back issues. Most newsstands will carry it. *Rolling Stone* will almost certainly contain material offensive to Christian readers.

Tapes

Beeman, Bob. *Hear No Evil.* P. O. Box 5592, Anaheim, CA 92806. This taped lecture by Bob Beeman contains useful information about rock music. Although not all Christians will agree with every statement, he takes a reasonably strong position against rock and includes musical examples of back-masking. Get the tape directly from Bob Beeman rather than through *Firefighters for Christ* (the name of the distribution organization that appears on the label). They promote neo-evangelical comedian Mike Warnke, whose "comedy" shows no reverence for the majesty and holiness of God.

Dobson, James. *Focus on the Family.* Box 500, Arcadia, CA 91006. Tape C82, "Christian Music in the Church and Home," features a panel discussion with several individuals active in contemporary Christian music. The most important of these is Michael Omartian, who has released a number of his own albums in the CCM field, while producing Donna Summer in the secular market. Also participating is John Styll, the publisher of *Contemporary Christian Magazine.* The discussion ends as a "draw," at best. Acting as the "devil's advocate," Dobson makes several good points concerning the problems of CCM. The CCM group admits its flaws, but no one comes out against Christian rock. The tape will help you know what CCM performers are thinking.

Appendix Four

Listening Suggestions

Lumpers and Dividers Briefly Revisited

We talked about "lumpers" and "dividers" in chapter two. The lumpers think all contemporary music is rock; the dividers try to divide and redivide contemporary music until they find a seemingly "acceptable" slice.

As a result, it is always interesting—in a strange way—to hear a rock fan say something like this: "Oh, I don't like classical music. It all sounds the same to me." That seems a lot like what you hear from the lumpers who think all rock is noise, doesn't it?

Even by saying "classical music," we are lumping together many different periods, each period characterized by a different type of music. But just as we decided to use "rock" in a general sense, we will use "classical music" in a conversational way to mean the music of this century and of centuries past that is studied and enjoyed by knowledgeable listeners.

The point is that, just as it isn't fair for critics to lump together all rock music as noise, it is equally unfair to make a general statement about classical music. Just as most of us do not find *all* types of contemporary music appealing, neither will we find *all* types of classical music appealing. However, there is far more classical music from which to choose. This makes it easier for us to find music we like—although it does take a little more effort than just turning on the radio.

Suggestions for Getting Started

Remember that people often like what they hear frequently. The chances are good that if you had grown up listening to classical music, you would already like classical music. If you didn't grow up with this music, here are some ways to get started.

1. Listen, listen, listen! You cannot merely listen to a piece of music once and make a fair decision about it. When you buy a record (or when listening to a record or tape you have borrowed from the library), plan to listen to it at least ten times before you decide anything about it.

2. Learn about the music. Many people who like contemporary music know a great deal about the music, or the performers, or both. To like classical music, you need to know about it. Of course, Satan will make sure that this is *not* as easy as learning about rock music—but you can learn! Begin with the record jacket. Even if you don't understand it all the first time through, read it. Then go to an encyclopedia and read about the composer. If you find that you especially like the piece of music, you may even want to go to the library and find a biography of the composer.

3. Buy or borrow a music appreciation textbook. It will describe the various periods and many of the composers. This information will enable you to get a broad overview of when the music was written, what the historical and cultural forces were that affected it, and more. Don't be afraid of words like "historical" and "cultural." Those same forces affect our music today. The problem is that many of the effects are increasingly sinful, and the Christian must not be associated with the music that results from such forces.

4. Attend live concerts. Just as your appreciation of contemporary music may have been enhanced by attending concerts, your appreciation for classical music will *certainly* be enhanced by hearing it performed live. As suggested in chapter ten, even the most confirmed rock fan will be impressed by the sound of a large orchestra in an acoustically good concert hall.

There is nothing "magic" about these suggestions. Nor will following four steps result in an instant love for classical music. In my own experience, developing a liking for classical music took months—in some ways, years. You should expect some struggle. When you seek to please God, Satan is sure to resist your efforts. You are not fighting merely your own desires, but the devil as well.

> For we wrestle not against flesh and blood, but against principalities, against powers, against the rulers of the darkness of this world, against spiritual wickedness in high places. Wherefore take unto you the whole armour of God, that ye may be able to withstand in the evil day, and having done all, to stand (Ephesians 6:12-13).

Ideas for Listening

Some give up rock and begin randomly buying classical records, hoping to find something they like. While their intention is good, most of us don't have enough money to "experiment." It is helpful to know a little about the music itself or about the composer.

This list gives you some basic information about a number of standard works. You should be able to find these in almost any large record store. Another alternative is to join a good mail-order record club. Two fine clubs that deal chiefly in classical music are:

International Preview Society
P.O. Box 91406
Indianapolis, IN 46291

Musical Heritage Society
1710 Highway 35
Ocean, NJ 07712

Obviously, the list reflects my own personal preferences, to some degree, and the preferences of others who assisted in its preparation. You may find you don't agree with every description or opinion expressed here. That's good; you will want to develop your own list of favorites. But for the reader without any background in classical music (and that was my own experience), the list will be a good guide and may even help save a considerable amount of time and money as you begin your musical explorations.

Keep in mind that these works will often be available on recordings by several different orchestras. Some of the pieces have also been transcribed and recorded both by orchestras and by solo pianists. After you find your own favorites, you may enjoy purchasing more than one version of the work and comparing the performances.

The selections marked with a star are recommended as especially good starters. As with the larger list, not all of these will become favorites, but you will almost certainly find some works that you like.

Very special thanks are extended to those who assisted with the preparation of this appendix. The basic list and annotations were provided by Bill and Joan Pinkston, along with additional suggestions made by Miss Judy Gamble. Without their help, the list would have reflected only my own preferences—and would therefore have been less comprehensive and much less useful to the Christian who is seeking to establish good music standards.

Brandenburg Concertos, Johann Sebastian Bach
The ruler of Brandenburg was impressed with Bach and asked him to write music for him. The result was the six *Brandenburg Concertos*. The orchestra is divided into two groups that are used in contrast to each other.

Orchestral Suite No. 3 in D Major, Johann Sebastian Bach
Bach wrote a large quantity of music during his long life. One of the most familiar is the beautiful and solemn "Air" from this suite.

Moonlight Sonata, Ludwig van Beethoven *
This is a slow, melodic piano piece that almost everyone will know.

Symphony No. 5, Ludwig van Beethoven *
Symphony No. 5 is the most famous major work of this well-known composer. Recurring themes make this piece an easy introduction to "classical music."

The Roman Carnival Overture, Hector Berlioz
This piece was written as the prelude to the second act of an opera, but today it is usually performed as a separate piece.

Symphonie Fantastique, Hector Berlioz
One writer described *Symphonie Fantastique* as a showcase for orchestra and a "fantasized autobiography in sound." Originally it was titled *Episode in the Life of an Artist* and was written to impress a young, Irish Shakespearean actress, whom Berlioz later married.

Polovetsian Dances, Alexander Borodin
Borodin wrote treatises on chemistry and lectured on medicine. He spent seventeen years writing an opera that he never finished. The *Polovetsian Dances* from this opera, however, is lively music that has earned Borodin a place in the history of music, even though his scientific efforts are forgotten.

Academic Festival Overture, Johannes Brahms
The University of Breslau conferred an honorary doctor's

degree on Brahms, who wrote and conducted the premier performance of this piece in the school's honor.

Hungarian Dances, Johannes Brahms
Brahms wrote these as piano duets. The original melodies are old folk songs. Brahms arranged several of them for orchestra, which is how we generally hear them today.

Piano Concerto No. 1 in D Minor, Johannes Brahms *
This is a strongly emotional work with a particularly lovely adagio (slow) movement. Highly recommended.

Piano Concerto No. 2 in B-Flat Major, Johannes Brahms *
This four-part concerto is beautiful music throughout. The piano and the orchestra weave rich melodies around each other.

Scottish Fantasy, Max Bruch *
When called by its full title, "Fantasy for Violin with Orchestra and Harp, freely using Scottish Folk-Melodies," this work is properly labeled. The music is lovely; the listener can almost visualize the ruins of an old castle. Highly recommended.

Violin Concerto No. 1 in G Minor, Max Bruch
This work demonstrates both the emotion of the composer and the virtuosity of the performing violinist. Bruch's works may be more difficult to find than others on this list, but they are worth the search because of their rich, brooding quality.

Appalachian Spring, Aaron Copland *
Written in 1944, this composition has many beautiful moments. The following description was in the program when the piece was first performed: "Spring was celebrated by a man and a woman building a house with joy and love and prayer; by a revivalist and his followers in their shouts of exultation; by a pioneering woman . . . ." Highly recommended.

Fanfare for the Common Man, Aaron Copland *
Fanfare is dramatic, "olympic-sounding" music. This relatively brief piece is a favorite of many.

Rodeo, Aaron Copland
Capturing sounds and excitement from the West, Copland has given us an entertaining work. You will hear "sound pictures" of exactly what you might expect from a work of this title.

New World Symphony (No. 5), Anton Dvořák
Called more correctly, *From the New World*, this work is an interesting description of America by a Czech who spent several years in the United States. Dvořák weaves several familiar tunes, including "Swing Low, Sweet Chariot," "Going Home," and "Hot Cross Buns," into this piece.

Peer Gynt, Suite No. 1, Edvard Grieg
Peer Gynt was a play, and this music was originally written to bridge scenes and to introduce acts. The play is all but forgotten, but Grieg's music is still popular. "Morning" and "In the Hall of the Mountain King" are both familiar sections.

Piano Concerto in A Minor, Edvard Grieg
Considered Grieg's masterpiece, he wrote this when he was only twenty-five. It has been described as a "burst of youthful ardor." It contains emotional, as well as hymnlike, passages.

Grand Canyon Suite, Ferde Grofé *
After a visit to the Grand Canyon, Grofé recorded his impressions musically in a series of movements entitled "Sunrise," "Painted Desert," "On the Trail," and "Sunset and Cloudburst." This is an exciting piece with much emotion and many "sound descriptions."

The Messiah, George Frederick Handel *
Probably the best known of all the oratorios, *The Messiah* has many familiar melodies and a text drawn from Scripture. Every Christian should be able to receive great spiritual benefit and encouragement from both the words and the music.

Water Music, George Frederick Handel *
In the 1700's, King George I of England held "water parties" during which his guests would be entertained on the water on large, flat barges. On one barge was a small orchestra. Handel's *Water Music* was written to be performed for these occasions. This is light baroque music with the sound quality one might expect at a court party.

The Planets, Gustav Holst *
Each planet is musically described in this unusual and dynamic piece. Many modern sounds and harmonies add to the excitement of this suite.

Hungarian Rhapsody (No. 2), Franz Liszt
Liszt wrote this piece for the virtuoso pianist, and it is at

its best when performed on the piano. There is also an orchestral setting of this popular piece.

Italian Symphony (No. 4), Felix Mendelssohn
Mendelssohn is supposed to have captured in his works the essence of various places he visited. The *Italian Symphony* brings Italy to the minds of some listeners; to others, it is merely beautiful music.

A Midsummer Night's Dream, Felix Mendelssohn
Originally written as incidental music to Shakespeare's play and later put together as a suite, this work, which includes the traditional "Wedding March," contains some of the most familiar music of the classics.

Eine Kleine Nachtmusik, Wolfgang A. Mozart
The title may be translated "a little night music." Mozart is known for elegance. This serenade for strings is for a festive occasion and shows the delicacy of eighteenth-century classical music.

Pictures at an Exhibition, Modest Mussorgsky *
An exhibition of the works of Victor Hartmann, a painter and architect, was held the year after his death. Ten of the works inspired his friend Mussorgsky to write a set of tone poems. Possibly the best known, "The Great Gate of Kiev," is a massive, impressive composition. Highly recommended.

Canon in D Major, Johann Pachelbel *
This music accompanies portions of one of the breathtaking films at the Smithsonian Air and Space Museum in Washington, D.C. It is a pleasant, easy-to-remember work that many enjoy.

Piano Concerto No. 2 in C Minor, Sergei Rachmaninoff *
Known for his soaring melodies and rich, lush sounds, Rachmaninoff is a favorite of many. This is one of his most popular pieces.

Sonatine and *Pavane pour une Infante Defunte,* Maurice Ravel *
This two pieces are music for the piano that is both elegant and moving. Orchestral recordings of the Pavane are also available. These brief works will likely be found on record in combination with others by Ravel. You may enjoy "Le Tombeau de Couperin" and other Ravel works as well. Highly recommended.

Pines of Rome, Fountains of Rome, and **Roman Festivals,** Ottorino Respighi *

This is brilliant, exciting music from the early 1900s. These pieces are tone poems describing sights in the city of Rome.

Capriccio Espagnole, Nicolas Rimsky-Korsakoff
Rimsky-Korsakoff first planned this piece as a violin fantasy on Spanish themes. It grew to a large orchestral piece that reflects the composer's view of that colorful country.

Scheherazade, Nicolas Rimsky-Korsakoff
The sultan boasts that none of his wives have ever been unfaithful to him for they have all been put to death after their wedding night. But Scheherazade tells the sultan a story on their wedding night and will not tell him the ending until the next night. She thus remains alive, as the piece says, "A Thousand and One Nights." The stories of Sinbad and Prince Kalendar come from this old collection of tales.

Concerto de Aranjuez, Joaquin Rodrígo *
Written in 1940, this guitar concerto features a rich orchestral score and guitar passages of great technical difficulty. Listen particularly to the adagio (slow) movement. Highly recommended.

The Organ Symphony (No. 3 in C Minor), Camille Saint-Saëns *
The Philharmonic Society of London commissioned Saint-Saëns to write this piece. Featuring two pianos and an organ, it is a dynamic piece that reaches grand proportions and a majestic finish.

Finlandia, Jean Sibelius *
At the end of the nineteenth century, Finland was seeking independence from Russia. Sibelius wrote this symphonic poem about his native country. One especially beautiful part of this work is the musical accompaniment for the hymn "Be Still My Soul."

The Moldau, Bedřich Smetana
The Moldau is a river in Bohemia. This piece describes a trip down the river from the beginning of the stream past cities, over rapids, by small villages, majestic castles, and finally out to sea. It is interesting to follow the piece, looking for these musical pictures.

The Blue Danube and *Tales from the Vienna Woods,* Johann Strauss
These are familiar works from Strauss. Both will be enjoyed by those who like the waltzes of this Austrian master.

Don Juan, Richard Strauss

Don Juan's storied exploits form the basis for this work.

Till Eulenspiegel, Richard Strauss
This symphonic poem describes the comic escapades of a legendary medieval rogue.

Firebird Suite, Igor Stravinsky
Stravinsky's work is a very dramatic piece, one that many enjoy. It is based on the old legend of the bird that dies in flames but arises from its ashes.

Light Cavalry, Franz von Suppé
This piece was first written for a comic operetta dealing with the military and has become a traditional spoof on military life.

1812 Overture, Peter Ilich Tchaikovsky *
This piece commemorates the Russian Battle of Borodino in 1812, which ended with Napoleon's flight from Moscow after the city was set aflame. Originally the work was to be performed in a public square in front of a cathedral. At the end of the piece, the bells of the cathedral and other bells of the city were to be rung and cannons to be fired. Although these sounds are only imitated for the concert hall or on recording, it makes for a stirring finish!

Nutcracker Suite, Peter Ilich Tchaikovsky
The overture is familiar to almost everyone. A number of other parts of this work will also be familiar, including the "Russian Dance" and "Waltz of the Flowers." Reading the story associated with this work and then listening to the music will help you enjoy this piece more.

Piano Concerto in B-Flat Minor, Peter Ilich Tchaikovsky
This is a brilliant piece that demands a skilled pianist. The familiar first theme has been "lifted" and used in more popular pieces than any other classical work.

Romeo and Juliet, Peter Ilich Tchaikovsky
This overture, based on Shakespeare's tale, has a familiar love theme. It also presents the contrasts of the two feuding families portrayed in the play.

Swan Lake and **Sleeping Beauty,** Peter Ilich Tchaikovsky
These two works offer exciting, beautiful music. Many of the themes are familiar, and the story is interesting to follow.

Aïda: Grand March, Giuseppe Verdi
Returning victorious to Egypt, the army marches into the city carrying the spoils and leading the prisoners to the accompaniment of this stirring march.

A Few Final Suggestions

Specific recordings have not been suggested for the works listed above for two reasons: first, many fine albums and tapes are available for most of these works. It would be counterproductive to list only one and cause you to pass up another equally fine recording. Second, records sometimes go "out of print" (are dropped by the company). As a result, only the works and the composers are shown above—in hopes of encouraging you to purchase and compare various recordings.

However, even at the risk of the following recordings becoming unavailable, at least four albums deserve to be mentioned as records of special interest to the Christian. You will find these worth seeking, in addition to the works listed above.

Christmas with the Canadian Brass, RCA ARL 1-4132
For the Christian, Christmas is a season of special remembrance of Christ. With the increasing number of records featuring hymns and carols set to rocklike background music, a recommendation for Christmas music seems appropriate. The sound and technical quality of this recording are first-rate, and the selections include many favorites.

Sacred Music for the Guitar, Christopher Parkening, EMI/ Angel Records DS-37335
Excellent guitar transcriptions played by an outstanding classical guitarist make this album a valuable addition to your collection. Highly recommended.

Stowkowski Conducts Bach, London Symphony Orchestra, RCA ARL 1-0880
Here are outstanding transcriptions of Bach for orchestra, including a fine version of EIN' FESTE BURG, the music to which Luther set the hymn "A Mighty Fortress Is Our God." Highly recommended.

Symphony of Praise, Bob Jones University Symphony Orchestra, Unusual Recordings, Stereo 018150
This record combines high-quality arranging and performance of some of the Christian's best-loved hymns and gospel songs. Highly recommended.

Indexes

Scripture Index

Rock and CCM Index

Songs, Albums, and Videos

Rock and CCM Groups and Performers

General Index